Common Sense Rules

What you really need to know
about business

Deborah Meaden

BUSINESS
BOOKS

Published by Random House Business Books 2009

2 4 6 8 10 9 7 5 3 1

First published in Great Britain in 2009 by
Random House Business Books
Random House, 20 Vauxhall Bridge Road,
London SW1V 2SA

www.rbooks.co.uk

Addresses for companies within The Random House Group Limited can be found at:
www.randomhouse.co.uk/offices.htm

The Random House Group Limited Reg. No. 954009

A CIP catalogue record for this book
is available from the British Library

ISBN 9781847940216 (Hardback edition)
ISBN 9781847940261 (Trade paperback edition)

The Random House Group Limited supports The Forest Stewardship
Council (FSC), the leading international forest certification organisation. All our
titles that are printed on Greenpeace approved FSC certified paper carry the FSC
logo. Our paper procurement policy can be found at
www.rbooks.co.uk/environment

Contents

Acknowledgements

Writing *Common Sense Rules* has been a challenging experience for me. Although I constantly retain specific nuggets of information and learn from past experiences, I confess that the anecdotes and context that make it interesting to people on the outside often slip my mind. I am, therefore, very grateful that ex-*Mail on Sunday* journalist Teena Lyons has helped me by jogging my memory and teasing out the relevant stories, which could not have been an easy task. I would also like to thank Sophie Lazar at Random House, who introduced me to Teena and who has worked so hard in overseeing the project.

My success over the years has in large part been due to the people around me. I like smart and challenging characters who are willing to take a risk, and am fortunate to have been constantly surrounded by them throughout my career. In the beginning it was Carlos Magello, who believed in me, despite my youth and relative inexperience, and awarded me the Stefanel franchise. Later it was John Mackie at Lloyds Bank who found a way to fund my buyout of Weststar, and there were many in between far too numerous to mention.

At Weststar I never failed to be impressed and inspired by my team at all levels, from the board through to the general managers who showed breathtaking entrepreneurial spirit in running the holiday parks, to the people on the ground who made every Weststar holiday special.

The team at Phoenix Equity Partners – and in particular, David Gregson, Sandy Muirhead, Steve Darrington and Andrew Deakin who led the Weststar buyout – have earned my respect for the intelligent and direct manner in which they work, and my thanks for convincing me to do something I had not previously wanted to do and then proving categorically that they were right to do so.

I cannot, of course, ignore *Dragons' Den*. My fellow Dragons constantly keep me on my toes because they are clever, competitive and challenging and I have been very lucky to know and work with them all. Helen Bullough and Dominic Bird on the production team, who first introduced me to the Den, deserve my particular thanks and respect, as do the many entrepreneurs who come on the programme. Whatever happens in the Den, the entrepreneurs have to be admired for having the strength and ambition to face the Dragons. My own investments, from the Den and elsewhere, should get a special mention too. I have thoroughly enjoyed working with them all and watching them grow into successful and admired entrepreneurial ventures.

My appreciation also goes to my family. I have always admired my parents Brian and Sonia for their direct, professional approach and the example they have set. I like the fact that they have never given me the easy way out. From an early age they expected a lot from me and showed me that if I wanted to achieve something meaningful then I had to do it for myself. I am very grateful for that. I am grateful to my sisters, too. Gail, herself a true entrepreneur whom I admire and whose judgement I trust totally, and Emma and Cass, all intelligent, capable and funny, have kept my feet firmly on the ground by never, ever cutting me any slack.

Finally, thank you to my husband Paul, who is as smart as can be. It can't be easy for a private man to live this life which straddles business and media, but with quiet confidence and amazing insight he supports me and keeps our life on track ... not always an easy task.

Introduction

Scarcely had I arrived at the studio for my first day on *Dragons'
Den* than I was ushered into make-up and told I was needed
straight away. Apparently, the producers had already had the sets
and lighting prepared and wanted to film me climbing the
wooden stairs to the Den. The idea was that I would be entering
the Den in precisely the same way as entrepreneurs who come on
the show seeking an investment and that, as a result, I would 'get
a feel' for the programme from all perspectives.

As I stood at the bottom of those stairs I became unusually
nervous for the first time since I had agreed to join the
programme. By the time I reached the top my heart was racing
and my ears were pounding, just as I suspect most entrepreneurs
feel as they enter the Den.

Looking back, I realise that although it was something of a
baptism of fire, the producers were right to get me used to the
environment early on because it quickly became apparent that
the other Dragons had no intention of cutting me any slack.
Everyone was polite and welcoming, but it was clear from the
outset that I was going to have to cut the mustard, or life in the

Den would be very difficult indeed. I was constantly being tested. I vividly remember making some comment or other and hearing Duncan pipe up, 'What Deborah means is . . .'. That was the moment to assert myself. I immediately pulled him up and told him – and of course everyone watching the show – that I was perfectly capable of explaining what I meant.

Everything that happened in those early days showed the truth of the unwritten rule that while entrepreneurs have to prove themselves to the Dragons, Dragons have to prove themselves to the other Dragons. After all, if a weak Dragon enters the Den all of our reputations are going to be spoiled.

Four series later, the rule still holds. The Den remains highly competitive, and our involvement in it resembles an endless fencing match. From my point of view that's exactly as it should be. After all, we never know who is going to come up those steps next or what scheme they are going to unveil. We all need to be able to react and to think on our feet in exactly the same way we do when we're running our various businesses. Challenges, opportunities and the unforeseen crop up the whole time, and we have to know how to deal with them effectively.

Since joining the programme's line-up I have sat through hundreds of pitches. Some of them have left me and my fellow Dragons hooting with laughter or fuming with frustration. Others have appealed to one or two of us, but not all. Just occasionally, though – perhaps once or twice in a series – a gem of a business idea emerges, and I can feel the mood in the Den lift. Suddenly, all five Dragons want a piece of the action, and the atmosphere becomes electric. As I've already said, we're all hugely competitive by nature, and when we see something really good none of us wants to lose out.

Two Den pitches particularly stand out in my mind. The first was a presentation early in series four by a pair from Watford, Alistair Turner and Anthony Coates-Smith. They were there to talk about Igloo Thermo Logistics, which delivers chilled and frozen foods to high-street stores. They had set up the company after working for Coca-Cola and Sainsbury's because they believed that the traditional 'white van man' style of customer service could be bettered.

Before they even formally launched into their presentation we all felt they were on to something. They clearly did, too, and were impressively confident. You could sense the excitement in the air. It emerged that they already had a working business model, and they explained this clearly and eloquently. More importantly, they both obviously understood what they needed to do in order to turn the model into reality and make their business a success. The reason they were standing in the Den, they explained, was because they had realised that they were at a stage where they could either do it the fast way, with Den investment, or the slow way, with finance from the bank. They wanted to do it the fast way. They wanted £160,000 for an 8 per cent stake in their business.

Even under some tough questioning they remained calm and confident, so it came as no surprise when we all put in a bid. Duncan Bannatyne and Richard Farleigh won by offering the lowest equity demand, and the rest, as they say, is history. Igloo has been enormously successful, just as we all knew it would be, and indeed, just months after the programme it was valued at £4 million.

The second pitch I particularly remember was by Gary Taylor of Alpine Cleaning Services, it was a pitch that came early on in my time in the Den. Gary wanted £200,000 for 20 per cent of his mobile truck and coach wash business. In some ways he could not have been more different from Alistair and Anthony: he was not particularly confident, and in the discussions we had with him he proved to be less articulate. However, he instantly convinced us that he knew his stuff.

His business idea was a brilliantly simple one. His meticulous research had revealed that the 450,000 lorries on British roads require cleaning about every ten days. Drivers of cars may be able to let things drift, but drivers of lorries are aware that their vehicles carry the logos of the companies they work for and that a clean lorry gives a good impression. In fact, Gary pointed out, it is a contractual obligation for trucks to look presentable, and drivers are given a budget for washing them at regular intervals. From this observation came an enticing business opportunity and one that Gary was determined to exploit.

He'd already made a strong start before he made his pitch to the Dragons, securing contracts with two out of the three major motorway services operators, Road Chef and Welcome Break, to set up a truck wash on their forecourts in 26 service stations. He had also had positive feedback from the 350 hauliers he had talked to when he was researching his idea. Moreover, he had established that his company, Alpine, needed to clean only two lorries an hour to break even. Why did he come to us? Well, he knew that he could secure the money he needed from the bank, but he was keen to get some real sales and marketing expertise on board to grow this remarkable business.

Peter Jones quickly dropped out, claiming it was not a viable business option. What followed next, however, was one of the fiercest bidding wars I have ever experienced in the Den.

Duncan kicked off by offering £100,000 for 20 per cent of the business, a sum quickly matched by Richard. Then Theo jumped in and offered a three-way split, adding up to 40 per cent of the business. When it came to me I offered the whole £200,000 for 40 per cent of the business. I absolutely did not want to work in a four-Dragon consortium and cautioned Gary that working with so many of us would be complete overkill and would over-complicate a good, simple business model. Duncan retorted by calling me a 'dirty little gazumper'. It was obvious that tensions were really high in the Den, but we were all clearly loving it. Alpine was a fantastic business opportunity and none of us was prepared to lose, but, boy, were we going to enjoy the battle of wills.

To add another layer of tension, Richard then changed teams and said he would go in with me, offering £100,000 for 20 per cent, if I would take the other half. I agreed. Now it was over to Gary. In case there was any doubt, I outlined his options and said I would not negotiate on my offer, so there was no point asking.

There was a long silence in the Den. After what seemed like ages, Duncan came up with a revised offer of £100,000 for a 17.5 per cent stake in Alpine. More silence. Then Richard said that he would switch sides to match Duncan's offer and join him in accepting a 17.5 per cent stake. Theo was left having offered £100,000 for 20 per cent, and we agreed that our offer would stand against Duncan's and Richard's.

Gary must have been in turmoil inside. But, admirably, he tried to keep negotiating, turning to Theo and me to ask us to put a 'bit of sweetness' back into the taste of the deal. By now, we really wanted that business, but we stood fast, and Theo repeated that 'the offer is the offer'. We would not negotiate. The deal was the deal. Gary could accept a lower stake, or he could take the considerable combined marketing and sales expertise of Theo and myself. It was a hugely tough decision, but eventually Gary chose to go with our deal. I was delighted – particularly when, after the usual round of hand-shaking and congratulations, Peter leaned over to me and whispered, 'That is the moment you proved yourself a Dragon.'

What's interesting about those two successful pitches is that, in some ways, they couldn't have been more different. The personalities involved contrasted strongly – the confident Alistair and Anthony, the more uncertain Gary. The Igloo Thermo Logistics entrepreneurs already had a strong background in the area of business they were planning to grow; Gary, on the other hand, was working from meticulous research. Nor were they seeking the same things. Alistair and Anthony wanted the Dragons to invest so that they could expand quickly. Gary was looking for outside sales and marketing expertise.

So what was the X factor in each case that got the Dragons so excited? It may come as a surprise if I say that it wasn't the business propositions in themselves that appealed. After all, lots of people have good ideas, and if the basis of *Dragons' Den* was simply to encourage bids for ingenious new inventions or businesses, most would probably attract some sort of investment. No, what appealed in both these cases were the people behind the idea. We realised as we spoke to them that they could think creatively, act decisively and overcome difficulties. These were entrepreneurs who were determined to make their business succeed, no matter what was thrown at them. Gary, for example, had to show that he could think on his feet. He was suddenly being offered two deals, one superficially more attractive than the other, and he had to weigh up the pros and cons of each in a matter of minutes. The fact that he went for the one that involved a sacrifice of a further 5 per cent of his business in return for what he instinctively knew he needed – sound sales and marketing advice – demonstrates his ability to think like an entrepreneur.

I am constantly asked if there is a blueprint for entrepreneurial success, and I always say, 'No, there isn't.' Every venture is unique, with its own opportunities and its own particular problems to solve and hurdles to overcome. As the experiences of Alistair, Anthony and Gary show, there isn't a single path to success – there are many. Nor, as the personalities involved in the two pitches amply demonstrate, are all entrepreneurs cast from the same mould.

Having said that, I do believe that there is a mindset that many entrepreneurs share, and exploring this mindset is one of the main purposes of this book. Put in a nutshell, the entrepreneurial mind is founded on that least common of commodities – common sense. Common sense involves knowing how to go about asking basic questions and anticipating challenges. It involves learning how to deal with inevitable setbacks and disappointments. And it tells you when you need to forge ahead and when you should cut your losses. It's not the easiest thing to acquire, but it is a skill you can hone and develop. True entrepreneurs never stop learning from their own successes and failures – and from one another.

At the same time, of course, there are many basic dos and don'ts in business, and so I have also set out to offer some practical advice on everything from setting up and running a business to selling it on. After all, there are some fundamental mistakes that you just don't need to make, and I hope that once you've read what I have to say, you never will.

In my own case, I think much of my success has come from taking nothing for granted and questioning absolutely everything, a philosophy I was already formulating when I was sent to boarding school at the age of seven. The school was in Wincanton, Somerset, and there were so many rules that I'm not convinced even the school authorities could remember them all. It was a small school with around 100 pupils between the ages of seven and 12. It wasn't a particularly posh or strict school, but I really resented the loss of freedom and independence, even at such a young age. I had always been an independent and self-reliant child and rebelled at what I considered to be pointless rules.

My first few years at the school were among the most miserable in my life, but I learned to navigate my way through the system and to channel my frustration into self-reliance. By sticking by the rules that I thought were sensible and completely disregarding the ones that I thought were stupid, I managed to resist the restrictive and linear approach the school so wanted me to have and adopt the more intuitive, free thinking and adaptable approach that I advocate here and that has stood me in such good stead in my business career. Along the way, I gained some relief from the daily grind by forcing exasperated teachers to explain why I should abide by what were clearly farcical regulations. My teachers must have found me a challenging pupil, but what I was developing were the habits of thought that have carried me through my years in business.

Today, more than ever, it is important to have creative entrepreneurs who know how to think for themselves. We are in the toughest economic climate that most generations have ever seen, but that doesn't mean that people should put their dreams on ice and wait until more buoyant times. True entrepreneurs have never been more relevant. Fortunes can – and will – be made in this recession because good entrepreneurs, with the right attitude and a brilliant idea, will not stop building successful businesses. Forged in the current climate, these ventures will be fundamentally far stronger than their counterparts that started in more prosperous times. I firmly believe that the pressure-cooker conditions of the recession will create some of the new household names of tomorrow. If even just one would-be entrepreneur is inspired by this book to turn their daydream into a reality, I shall feel I have done my job.

Chapter 1
What makes an entrepreneur?

Many people dream of starting up their own business, and any one of them may turn their great idea into a million-pound brand, but what separates the people who succeed from those who don't? Is it their background? It's certainly the case that many entrepreneurs who have built up large businesses (and who often have an ego to match) like to tell tales of how they struggled against adversity. They come up with unlikely stories of how they grew up sleeping rough in a rolled-up newspaper and yet somehow broke away from this wretched poverty and misery to become the businessman or woman they are today. They would have us believe that their desperately sad childhood spurred them on to succeed against the odds. Of course, it makes a great story, but ultimately it is just that: a story.

Common sense tells me there's a lot more to explain there. Plenty of people have tough starts in life and never recover. Equally, there are plenty of extremely successful entrepreneurs who benefited from comfortable upbringings and expensive educations. So does it just come down to luck? Are successful entrepreneurs just in the right place at the right time?

Personally, I don't believe in luck at all. People who appear to be lucky, who always seem to succeed at everything they do, simply work harder than the rest. Forget about being in the right place at the right time. People who make their own luck know which place to be and when to be there. They have the drive to succeed and an entrepreneurial spirit; they know how to make things happen because they know that the success or failure of their business is always down to them.

It's not where you come from, it's where you're heading

Entrepreneurs come from all walks of life, and you only have to look down the row of Dragons in the Den to realise that. There is Peter Jones, a gifted junior county tennis player, who, after a couple of early business setbacks, founded the hugely successful Phones International Group, which was at one time one of the fastest-growing businesses in Europe. Theo Paphitis was born in Cyprus and started his career as a tea boy with Lloyd's of London insurance before setting up his own company at the age of just 23 specialising in corporate turnarounds of ailing companies, such as Ryman the stationer and the Contessa and La Senza lingerie chains. James Caan's entrepreneurial spirit matches his father's, a man who worked day and night to set up a leather-trading business after moving to London from Pakistan in the 1960s. James, who left school when he was 16, set up the Alexander Mann Group, a leading recruitment company. And finally there's Duncan Bannatyne, who, after a poverty-stricken childhood, turned a £450 ice-cream van into a lucrative business, which in turn was invested to create a multimillion-pound nursing-home group and health-club chain.

My own upbringing was not exactly conventional, and it was certainly not steeped in cash and good fortune, but what it did give me was a good grounding in business pretty much from day one.

When I was very young, maybe just five or six years old, I worked alongside my sister Gail in a variety of businesses. In fact, by the time I was ten I had already chalked up stints counting money in an amusement centre, stocktaking in a chemist shop and handing out tickets at a bingo hall – more business experience than some people get in a lifetime.

Our early entry into the world of work came because my mother, Sonia, was at that time bringing us up on her own. My parents, who had married young, split up when I was just two. My mother fought tooth and nail to keep Gail and me with her, and at times it was clearly a struggle. She often did not have enough money to feed herself and went without so we could eat properly.

She was an inspiring presence in my childhood, showing resilience and fortitude that sparked off generosity in others. One particularly harsh winter we were staying in freezing cold, leaky-roofed accommodation in Clacton-on-Sea, Essex. My mother wanted to find us somewhere warm to live during the bleaker months and after much searching found a small flat, but her next hurdle was that she had no money to put down as a deposit. Unwilling to throw in the towel, she went to see a local lawyer to ask if there were any schemes that would allow her to borrow the cash. She was utterly determined to pay the money back but had no idea where to go to get an advance.

The lawyer, John Daldy, was a kind man with a quiet voice and a soothing smile. Sensing Sonia's desperation, he said he would see what he could do and asked politely if she would mind coming back the next day. When my mother did duly return John Daldy greeted her warmly, with a huge smile on his face, saying he had excellent news. He explained that he had managed to track down a little-known, government-backed scheme that would loan her the money on the proviso that she paid it back at the rate of £1 a week. My mother was overjoyed, and we rented the lodgings. She kept to her word and paid back every penny.

More than 20 years later Sonia discovered that this loan scheme had never existed at all. John Daldy, a complete stranger who had until that day never seen her before in his life, had loaned her the money out of his own pocket. He had seen a proud and honest young woman, who had been dealt a bad hand and who was doing everything in her power to keep her family together. I like to think that the kindness of this remarkable man was repaid, because he remained our family lawyer for years after that and his practice grew along with the success of our various family concerns. For a time, he even acted as the legal representative for the family company, Weststar, before he eventually retired.

Not that long after we moved into our rented home my mother received a call from Billy Butlin, who was then setting up his new Butlins holiday camp in Minehead, Somerset. She had been running a shooting range for him at his Clacton camp, and he was looking for people he could trust and respect to run concessions at the new location.

Because there was no money to pay for a childminder, my mother would take us into work with her. She could have given us colouring books, put us on stools in the corner of the room and asked us to keep quiet. But she was not like that. Because of her no-nonsense approach, which is, perhaps not surprisingly, very similar to my own, she believed that if we had to be there it would be better – and frankly more interesting – to make ourselves useful and engage with what was going on. She expected a lot from us, and it never occurred to us not to deliver.

An experience like this, helping out in my mother's business from such a young age, had a profound effect on me. Later, when my mother met Brian, who went on to become my stepfather and whom I now cherish as if he were my own father, the pair of them went into business together and became a formidable team who turned our lives around through hard work, good judgement and a great deal of courage. So, my formative years were spent either in the workplace itself or listening to intense conversations about business over the kitchen table. Business is in my blood. It has always been an important and ever-present part of my life.

I suppose you could say, looking at my upbringing, that I was always headed for a life in business – the path was clearly laid out, after all. However, it was my decision alone to pursue a career in business. And it had to be. To run a business you need to be committed, creative and driven. Anyone who feels they have been forced into it will not be able to give it their all. In a family business it is often taken as read that the younger generation will be willing to step up to the plate once the parents retire. However, younger generations often feel that the business of succession is actually a huge burden: many worry that they simply are not up to it or are not interested in business at all. Some will naturally want to be in business, but the others will just hate it. In my own family we have all followed very different paths. To succeed in business you have to do more than just be there. You have got to love every minute.

The elements of entrepreneurial spirit

Thanks to *Dragons' Den*, I've been fortunate enough to meet hundreds of entrepreneurs, with an incredibly wide range of personalities. Yet, the ones who truly inspire my Den colleagues and me and who get us reaching for our wallets all share a remarkably similar set of values. Ian Chamings, the man behind mixalbum.com, the music download website powered by the world's first automated DJ, is a good example. He presented his idea in series three of the programme, and it was clear from the start that he had something special. His product, mixalbum.com, allows you to choose your favourite dance tracks online and then ask an automated DJ to mix them at the touch of a button. It is unlike other music download sites where you pay just to download each track because this one professionally mixes them together so each one blends seamlessly into the next.

What Ian managed to get across very well in his pitch was that he had a great combination of skills. He was obviously very bright, with a highly logical and enquiring mind that was always looking

Seek out opportunity and seize it

for an opportunity. He hadn't just invented his product and then looked to see if there was a market. Instead, he was already plugged into his sector, had spotted a gap and decided to sort it out. I also liked the fact that although he seemed quite fearless and was clearly prepared to do what it takes to get his business off the ground, he was fully aware not only of the upside but also of the downside risk. If he doesn't know something, he will go and find out. He will also talk to anyone about anything if he thinks it will further his product. Best of all, he has the type of brain that, when it is presented with a problem, will immediately respond with a 'Right, how can I resolve this?' Far too many people come up against an obstacle and just freeze. What Ian had done was spotted an opportunity and seized it – the first step to becoming an entrepreneur – and what enabled him to take things to the next level was a combination of characteristics that I think are key to becoming a success.

Passion, focus and an insatiable desire to succeed

I've grouped these three qualities together because in my experience the way they interact is fundamental. I'm reminded of a really impressive entrepreneur I met in series six of *Dragons' Den* called Samantha Gore. Samantha was undoubtedly one of the brightest people to have graced the Den, and she was pitching her Saboteur Crime Prevention products. She had a great brain and could show an impressive track record because she was already running a string of successful businesses. By all accounts the Dragons should have bitten her hand off to invest. Yet, to this day

I have no idea what the products were that she was actually presenting. She was nervous and unfocused. I was left with the uncomfortable feeling that she may be one of my greatest ever missed investment opportunities, but her pitch was so awful I was left utterly exasperated by the experience. Samantha clearly had passion and a desire to succeed, but because she lacked focus I couldn't sensibly invest.

Of course, I have also found that some entrepreneurs have just too much focus and are so busy telling the Dragons the minutiae of how their inventions work that they somehow fail to mention what it actually does or even is. Towards the end of series three Richard Chadwick came on the show and spent a good hour talking about this massive Skyrota windmill that was dominating the set. He seemed to be saying that it presented a major innovation in wind turbines because it was small enough to fit on a domestic roof, giving homeowners free electricity and thus releasing them from the burden of spiralling utility costs. Then, a long way into the pitch, just as some of us were beginning to buy into the idea, it emerged that what he was actually selling was an extremely highly geared gearbox, which drove the windmill. His Tricom gearbox, which converts the slow-moving rotor speed of the turbine into a more efficient speed, was the tiny box sitting on the table beside him, which had gone completely unnoticed through the entire presentation. By that stage we were so baffled about what it was we were actually supposed to be investing in, it is hardly surprising that no one made an offer. Had we grasped what it was he was selling, our questions would have been different and so might the end result have been.

In another instance David Field and Ali Kord appeared in the

Den in series five with '3D heckler', a modern version of a puppet theatre. It was all to do with motion-capture technology: you put on a headscarf and glove and moved around and your image appeared as an animated puppet on a video screen. It was clearly a very clever device, but, other than limited use as a promotional tool, I just could not see that there would be enough potential customers. To make matters worse, David kept saying, 'There are hundreds of applications.' To which I repeatedly replied, 'Then give me an example of just one!' But he seemed unwilling – or unable – to do so and again left the Den empty-handed.

So, as you can see, having just some of the characteristics of passion, focus and a desire to succeed is not enough. An entrepreneur has to have them all and in the right proportions.

The beauty about having these qualities is that they take care of a lot of the other aspects of being an entrepreneur that people can find daunting. Far too many people are held back by their fear that they are not a born salesperson. I suspect that the multitude of entrepreneurs who tell me they 'can't sell' are actually very good salespeople. If they are as passionate about what they do as they should be it follows that they can't help but sell their dream to other people. Even if they do not consider themselves in the traditional mould of a salesperson that passion will naturally come out, and they'll be able to convince not just their customers, but also their staff, their bank manager and their investors.

Intelligence

An entrepreneur has to be quick-minded and bright. That doesn't mean they need to have gone to a top-notch public school, have a string of qualifications and be clever in an academic way. No. Rather, they must be clever in a quick-witted way, with a mind that refuses to accept barriers and that can solve a multitude of problems within seconds. Being quick-witted means that they are likely to be perceptive too, a quality that I think is absolutely vital in business.

Having the right intelligence for business means being able to think on your feet quickly and work under pressure. When there is a crisis business leaders can't say, 'I need to retire quietly into a corner for an hour or two to think about a solution.' They have to have the type of intelligence that kicks into action immediately after something has happened. They need to jump right into questions such as, 'What do I do?' or 'How do I fix this?' Anyone who goes into close-down at this point is in trouble.

Some people might say that the format of the Den is not a natural or fair way to judge whether an entrepreneur can think on their feet. It can, I know, seem quite brutal. But there is a reason for this. Generally, when investors in the outside world are weighing up whether to put money into a business, they might visit the premises, see the company in action and meet all the people involved before the entrepreneur even starts the pitch. The Dragons don't have that luxury. We have a short space of time to judge whether we are going to invest our own money in this person whom we have never met before. Consequently, the environment of the Den is designed to tell us more about a person than just how they present their business. It shows how they react under pressure and respond to the unexpected. It shows whether or not they are holistic thinkers.

What do I like to see in the Den? How do I judge intelligence? I like people who listen to my questions and give considered, knowledgeable and honest responses. Sometimes I'll ask what I call sidewinder questions, which tend to arise from what is being left unsaid. If there are some clearly important gaps in their pitch I want to know why they are steering away from the obvious. But sometimes, even when there are no obvious gaps in the pitchers' thinking, I like to throw in a sidewinder question just to see how they handle it. If they blurt an answer straight back and there is the merest whiff of bullshit, I don't consider that a good sign.

In series three of the *Den* Steve Johnston came on the programme to pitch StoryCode.com, a new website for books. The site was a combination of TripAdvisor and Amazon, where the user could choose the books and rate them. Personally I thought that the whole idea was crazy, but Steve had a confident sales pitch and an answer for absolutely everything. Every time he was thrown a question he instantly came back with an answer. I don't think it was *the* answer, but it was certainly *an* answer. I remember thinking at the time that I would be much more convinced if I could see him thinking about the questions for a moment so that I could be sure he had come up with a proper and considered response.

I had quite a few reservations about the proposition. I couldn't see what incentive there would be for someone who had read a book to go back on the website and put up a review. Equally, there didn't seem to be any mechanisms in place to show whether any good reviews were actually from the publisher or to highlight or soften a negative review on, say, a science fiction book from someone who clearly hated the genre. Yet, Steve Johnston had a quick-fire answer for every one. I got the feeling he was responding without really thinking. Indeed, he even blurted out the rather patronising phrase, 'I don't know if you read, Deborah.'

Well, yes, I can and indeed do. A lot. That comment was, of course, a fatal error because by then I was absolutely certain I would not invest. Thinking on your feet, while important, can be dangerous if you do not exercise a degree of intelligence and foresight to support it.

It works the other way, too. Another sign of an entrepreneur intelligence is the questions they ask and the way they gather knowledge from others. Take networking, for example, which is important, particularly in the early days, because it is a useful way to get knowledge from people who have experienced the market at first-hand or who have great contacts. But there has to be a specific purpose to networking because it can be incredibly time-consuming and mentally exhausting. It can be dangerous – and, frankly, a bit of a waste of time – to ask too many people about their experiences of setting up businesses, to give one example. I liken that to listening to stories about other people's trips to the dentist. It is not necessarily relevant because everyone has a different experience, and if you listen for too long about what a horrible time they had, odds on you will never go again.

Rather than spending hours comparing experiences and swapping tales of doom, I would much prefer to see people just getting on with it.

Spend your time wisely

Networking comes into its own when it is asking specific and knowledgeable people for advice about key aspects of the business. I would target individual people who may help the business, ring them up and ask if they have time for a coffee or to talk something over. Be specific and honest about what you want to find out, how much of their time you will need and stick to it. I am constantly being asked for five minutes of my time, which can mean anything up to an hour. Busy people are usually good time managers and have little time in their day to waste.

Thanks to *Dragons' Den* I am, of course, in a privileged position now, but long before I became well known I had no hesitation whatsoever about picking up the phone. I just thought, 'What do I need to know and who do I need to ask?' People don't mind being asked as long as the purpose is clear and the questions are succinct and targeted. Even today, if I have the time, I will help. If I am too busy, then I won't, but like most business people I will probably refer enquirers on to someone who will.

Sometimes I have been asked for advice in the most unusual of circumstances. For example, in the summer of 2008, while I was in the lift at the TV production company Endemol, a bright and confident young lady, Lucy Buck, asked if she could do an elevator pitch to me. Lucy, a TV producer, was setting up a charitable trust to build a home in Uganda for abandoned babies. As we travelled down five floors she explained how, through the Child's i Foundation, she intended to raise £1 million in just six months. I asked her to send me details of her proposals and said I'd be in touch.

Lucy had a specific problem and she needed advice. Although everything was ready for the launch date of the Child's i

Foundation website, for technical reasons it was some weeks off from being able to accept cash on its Justgiving account. Lucy had devised a 'buy a brick' application that would allow donors to buy a virtual brick to help build the home, and yet there were no means to accept the donations.

I picked up the phone to call her and pass on my advice, which amazed her. I told her that while I would normally strongly advise any company against launching a website before consumers are able to hand over their money (otherwise would-be customers become frustrated and leave, never to return), in this case I believed there should be an exception to the rule. If the charity's aim is to build a worldwide community of supporters, she would be well placed to begin immediately and then launch the build-a-brick facility at a later stage. When it comes to charity, people are much more willing to be patient than on a commercial site, sometimes even leaving their names and addresses for future contact.

The phone call took just 20 minutes of my time, but it made a big difference to Lucy.

Networking has a purpose, but it is not just to meet as many people as possible because one day they might be needed. This is why so-called 'networking groups' for fledgling entrepreneurs bother me. Generally, they are made up of a group of people looking for other people to network with. There is not enough time to do that. Remember, too, that networking is a two-way street, and anyone attending an event will be expected to give as good as she or he gets and the amount of time needed for all this can soon spiral out of control.

Similarly, clubs for entrepreneurs have mushroomed over the

past few decades. It is nice to know how other entrepreneurs think, but clinging to, or becoming dependent on, these clubs shows a lack of confidence. In fact, I can see more harm than good coming out of regular meetings of clubs of entrepreneurs. True entrepreneurs really don't need them. If someone has done the correct market research and is convinced that their product is right they should get on and do it. They will find their own way. They don't need to ask someone else to tell them how to do it. If they did so, that would mean they are not a leader. It would also mean they are actually looking for someone to give them a sense of direction.

Confidence and self-belief

Confidence attracts. We all look for it, and we can't help but follow it. It is one of humankind's basic instincts to look for somebody who is confident and comfortable in what they are doing. Even in the animal world it is the confident one that tends to dominate the pack. It is nothing to do with being the biggest or the most attractive. We all, instinctively, choose to follow the most confident person because they look as if they know what they are doing.

Most people can sense confidence. I can name most of my confident friends, even though many of them are really quite quiet people. They don't have to make a noise, and they don't have to tell everybody how fantastic they are. They just are, and they don't care what anybody else thinks. This is not just my personal belief. I have noticed in my business life that a confident person who doesn't feel the need to explain themselves can create a powerful reaction.

A good example is a business leader like Sir Gerry Robinson, who has led blue-chip British businesses from Grand Metropolitan to Granada and chaired British Sky Broadcasting, Allied Domecq and ITN. He is undoubtedly talented and knowledgeable, and I particularly like his philosophy that says that the skills required to run a business are relatively simple. But there is something else about him too. In a low-key, yet impactful way, he is confident and charismatic. He is someone who can get things done and he knows it.

If you are naturally confident it can be easier to make things happen. But for many people confidence comes from feeling in control or knowing where they're going next. It's unsurprising, then, that a lack of confidence is one of the key reasons for scores of ideas never making it off the ground. Not long ago a taxi driver spent a considerable time telling me how he came up with the idea of putting advertising boards in the back of taxis. As we crawled through London's evening traffic, he told me how he thought of doing it 15 years ago but failed to get it off the ground as a viable business.

'Look at it now,' he said, waving his hand at all the other cabs sitting in a stationary queue beside us. 'They are everywhere, and I bet my idea has made some lucky bloke millions.'

This cab driver is not alone. The world is full of people who have come up with spectacular ideas and failed to do anything about them. Often, without a trace of irony, they will tell you of the product's subsequent success in another person's hands as proof that they were on to a good thing all along. Part of the problem is a lack of self-belief. People don't know how to do it and don't think they can do it either. So they don't bother. It is generally much easier to do nothing about a good idea than it is to try something and fail.

Self-belief and self-reliance are quite hard to force if they don't come naturally, but even if someone is not naturally confident there are things they can do to help themselves. Clearly identifying what needs to happen next, for example, might help, as will pinpointing what skills are already there that can be applied to getting the business off the ground. Having a supportive family does make a difference too – after all, bringing up a confident child is all about supporting a child's confidence.

Instead, what usually happens is that everyone says, 'I don't know what to do next.' Getting through the bit they think they can't do is just too enormous a problem to overcome. Everybody has at least a few great ideas, but it is all too easy not to do something about them. It is simple to slip into a routine so that the years roll by and the ingenious idea gathers dust in the shed. It is, after all, much harder work actually to do something about an idea, and it takes a considerable amount of courage.

To be fair, many would-be entrepreneurs do try to take their idea beyond the garden-shed stage. They may show their plans to an engineer or an adviser in order to get it to the next stage. Yet, sadly, many of these brave souls fall by the wayside because they accept too readily the reply that their concept is 'not possible'.

A true entrepreneur would not accept that. There is always a way, and everything can be done. Unless it is actually against the laws of physics, it should be possible to find a route around something to get to a chosen point.

Look at it from another angle. When was the last time you physically couldn't do anything? I don't mean a point in your life where you stopped something because other considerations were in your way. I mean a time when you could not find a solution to a problem that you really had to solve. It is rare. Often when outsiders say something is impossible, it means they themselves do not have the know-how or they can't be bothered to think around the problem. The response might even be to cover their embarrassment at their own lack of knowledge. It is much easier to say 'It's not possible' than 'I don't know', and that reply does not expose their weaknesses. I would never accept that. Usually, when I hear the words 'I cannot do that', they are followed by the swift and sharp riposte, 'So find me someone who can.'

Commitment

It takes a lot of time and energy to be an entrepreneur. You have to be totally committed, and if there is the slightest inkling that you are not committed, everybody, including the market, will know. The ability to commit is not simply a state of mind; it is a core character trait.

Being committed means that the business comes first, at times to the exclusion of all else, even family and close friends. All of my dear friends, and I have many lifelong friends, will describe times in our lives when I have neglected them badly, and

I often feel incredibly fortunate still to be able to count them among my friends. But even when you accept that your business comes first and you are completely committed to it, it is important to apply your common sense. Just because you are 100 per cent committed doesn't mean that you're going to be able to operate at 100 per cent – or even 110 per cent, as many people have said to me – all the time. I've lost count of the number of earnest and enthusiastic entrepreneurs who have stood in front of me and vowed to 'give it 110 per cent'. This is one of the most overworked business clichés of this decade. I've bad news for anyone who believes that working hard and putting in long hours show their commitment to their entrepreneurial venture and who thinks that alone will bring success. You cannot give 110 per cent. Apart from being a mathematical impossibility, giving even 100 per cent is simply not realistic all of the time.

Entrepreneurs must be fighting fit to cope with every high and low that their business will throw at them – even more so during an economic slump – so they have to allow themselves some downtime. If they don't, they will simply not be ready for the moments when they have to give their absolute all.

Entrepreneurs who declare that they will keep themselves at that heightened '110 per cent' tension every single working day are talking nonsense. It is hugely frustrating to see people going into their workplace every Sunday 'to do stuff'. They believe that by making this sort of sacrifice they deserve to be successful. But if only it were that easy. Working smart, keeping yourself business fit, bringing yourself to peak condition when it is needed and slowing down for rest time when it is possible are far more effective.

If entrepreneurs truly understand their business and know what it needs they will see clear opportunities for down time. Trust me, there are going to be some days when there is not a lot to do. Not every day is going to be a fast-paced, frenetic round of deals and challenges. More to the point, it shouldn't be. Every business has its ebbs and flows. There should be times when someone heading a business will think, 'I am just going to step back because, boy, am I going to have to put my foot back down on the accelerator at certain periods.' When an entrepreneur can see the possibility for down time they should take it. When there is no down time available, they should give their business whatever it takes – and that may well be 100 per cent of their time and effort.

Loss averse

Being loss averse is nothing like being risk averse. It is about hating to lose. I loathe losing and am a terrible loser. However, I am careful not to show the outward signs of this character trait because I know it can be pretty unattractive, but I don't always succeed.

Not long ago I celebrated New Year with close, long-term friends in a charming country pub in Somerset. It was a lovely and convivial evening, full of laughter, jokes about old times and catching up on what had happened in the previous year. Then someone had the fateful idea of playing a round of 'pull the name out of the hat'. The rules are that everyone writes down the name of a famous person, folds their piece of paper and pops it in the hat. A member of the first team pulls out a name and mimes it. If someone on the same team correctly guesses the celebrity, they hold on to the hat and take out the next name and so on. The team with the most correct answers wins the game.

I was immediately alert and ready to play to the full. The fact that it was decided that the teams would be women versus men added to my feeling of competitive excitement. Sadly though, from the start, the men did not seem to share my view. They spent most of the time larking around and barely even attempted to make a serious effort. I gradually grew more and more riled, putting down their lack of fervour to the fact they were being churlish at losing and spurring on my team members not to get distracted by their childish posturing.

Eventually, one of my male friends lit a match and, with a flourish, threw it into the middle of the hat, setting the remaining pieces of paper ablaze. My reaction has become well known among my friends and family. Without hesitation I threw a glass of water into the hat and began drawing out the smouldering pieces of paper and blowing on them frantically, all the while shrieking at my by now bemused team-mates to continue because the names were still legible and urging them not to be put off by the poor sportsmanship of our menfolk. Hardly surprisingly the game was declared over (although I know we would have won), and I have never played it again since.

Losing in any circumstances, business or personal, makes me angry with myself and makes me resolve to do things better next

Take calculated risks – don't gamble

time. I don't mind taking risks, but with every potential risk I am constantly weighing up the potential outcomes. I ask myself if this is a risk worth taking? How likely is it that I will lose? If I am already losing, I weigh up whether I am likely to lose any more. It is the loss that bothers me, not the risk.

Entrepreneurs are prepared to take risks, but they're not gamblers. In fact, the idea of gambling is anathema to me. I cannot comprehend that there could be any pleasure to be found in a situation where I would have absolutely no control over the result. As a breed, entrepreneurs are prepared to take big risks, but we have calculated the outcome against the potential reward and would never dream of leaving it all to luck.

Over the years in the Den I have met some people I felt had not got their calculations right when it came to the risks they were taking. Nick Nethercott, a Gloucestershire-based entrepreneur who kicked off series three, was pursuing his dream of launching what was essentially a high-tech coffee table. Think of the Pac-Man and Space Invaders tables that dominated pubs in the 1980s and you would not be far off. Nick wanted £150,000 for 25 per cent of this business, claiming that the tables, which were priced at between £2,900 and £5,000, would be a hit in both a corporate and a domestic environment.

None of the Dragons was convinced. I told him that I had never reached such a quick conclusion in my life about not investing in a business. Companies have been trying to revive the gaming table concept for more than two decades and have not had a sniff of interest even when they are packaged for the retro market. But when he revealed that he was in the process of selling his house to get the dream off the ground, despite having two dependents, our jaws dropped. Not only was it a seemingly ludicrous idea, but he was also putting his whole family on the line for something that we thought did not stand a chance of succeeding.

No matter how compelling the dream, people do need to consider their circumstances and the consequences before they do anything. There are certain moments in a person's life when, I would say, no matter how much of an entrepreneur they believe themselves to be, they shouldn't do it. If there is a new baby on the way, a dramatic downturn in domestic fortunes or other unrelated reasons why their mind might be elsewhere, they shouldn't do it. I would say to them: 'You'll be able to follow your dream one day, just not right now.'

I would also say – and this is particularly pertinent in the current economic climate – that starting a business should never be a last-ditch solution for someone who is out of work. If someone is made redundant, thinking there are no better ways to raise cash is the worst reason in the world to set up a company. That new venture would be doomed from the start. However, if someone who has been thinking for years, 'I would love to build this idea into a business, or own a pub, or take on that franchise,' redundancy could be just the catalyst they need. As long as there is an idea, the mindset and the enthusiasm, a would-be entrepreneur will be off to a good start.

Being made redundant can be a really good catalyst for following a long-cherished dream, but what if you still have a job but want to start up a business? Many people are counselled by small-business advisers and bank business units to mitigate the risk by keeping their own jobs in the early stages of setting up their business, just in case it doesn't work out. In most cases this is not a good idea. It is fine to keep a job if it fits in with the new business, but keeping your job 'just in case' sends out a terrible message, suggesting as it does that you are not really convinced that your new business will work and displaying what can legitimately be seen as a serious lack of confidence.

As long as the plan is well thought through, entrepreneurs should be prepared to take a risk. If they are not 100 per cent convinced that their business is going to work, why are they even bothering? It is that simple. Doing half one job and half another, and keeping a foot in both camps, sends out the wrong signals to everybody. I would struggle to invest in entrepreneurs who thought they were going to keep their day job until they had a foothold in the market, unless they could clearly demonstrate the advantages. The most likely outcome will be that they will get to the stage when they suddenly realise it is all too much like hard work and run back to their safe environment. I have seen it happen hundreds of times.

If you are going to start a business, take it seriously. If you have done your calculations in a cool-headed and realistic way and still believe the risk is worth it, it probably is.

The habit of taking calculated risks is not a matter of being overly cautious and it sits well alongside the entrepreneurial desire to push the boundaries of everything after having weighed up all the options. Once one aspect of the business succeeds and the formula is proved right, new risks are constantly recalculated.

When I was 21 years old I bought the franchise for the Italian fashion and footwear company Stefanel in partnership with a friend. It was one of the first in the UK. However, although it taught me a great deal about retail and franchising and was enormously successful, I understood very quickly that I wanted more out of my career. Within just a few years I took the decision to sell my share in the venture to my partner because I realised that it would never be enough for me. I was quickly ready to move beyond my initial calculations of risk and explore new challenges.

If you watch entrepreneurs, you will see they are constantly looking around them, recalculating and coming up with ideas of how things can be done better. I must be a nightmare for my husband, Paul. As soon as we have done something, even as mundane as reorganising a cupboard, it does not have an hour to settle before I pipe up, 'But what if we did it this way?' It drives him bananas, but that is the nature of entrepreneurs. They are constantly looking to do better whether it's at work, home or play.

Realism

One of the strengths of *Dragons' Den* is that it exposes entrepreneurs to a dose of realism. Too many people convince themselves of the fantasy that their winning idea will make them a millionaire. They become swayed by their own customer research, during which they might have asked family or friends questions like, 'What do you think of this fabulous widget?' Invariably they get the answer 'It's brilliant!' But how often does our aspiring entrepreneur follow through with important questions such as 'Would you buy it?' and, crucially, 'How much would you pay?'

Entrepreneurs should always ask a full set of questions and not just come up with a load of research that 'proves' what they already think. Above all, though, they should be realistic. For example, while a lot of inventions may well do the job they set out to do, is the job they do enough to inspire people to shell out their hard-earned money? I am thinking here specifically of the Q-Top, which was presented to the Den by Roark McMaster in series three. Roark was pitching for an investment of £40,000 for a stake in a curious-looking, green plastic cover designed to protect and preserve cucumbers and lemons better than cling film or kitchen foil.

It is quite probable that many people have gone to the fridge with the remainder of a cucumber and thought, for a fleeting moment, 'Wouldn't it be good if there was a lid?' The question is, though, are they prepared to follow that thought through by going to the effort of tracking one down in the shops or on the Internet and then paying £4.99 for it? Yes, the Q-Top is a good idea, but there just really isn't enough of a pressing need for a cucumber lid.

People often mistake solving a problem with coming up with a great invention. If it is not a big enough problem people are not going to bother buying a product to solve it.

Similarly, an invention that requires consumers to change their behaviour radically is going to struggle in the marketplace. What we want is to find something to help us do what we already do better or more quickly rather than having to adapt our behaviour to make an invention work. Asking a market to change completely the way it behaves is unrealistic.

Inventor Peter Davis seemed to be asking consumers to do just that when he appeared in the Den in series three with his Axis Keyboard. The keyboard was like nothing I have ever seen: it had clusters of hexagonal notes rather than the usual piano-style linear keyboard we're all familiar with. Apparently, it was all about sound geometry, but the obvious flaw was it relied on everyone changing the way they played, while offering no real advantages.

As well as being realistic with their ideas, entrepreneurs should be realistic with themselves. Of course, the dream is to make loads and loads of money, but it's also important to enjoy the ride. As a business gains momentum it's worth asking yourself if you are actually making the dream happen. Is it really, really exciting? Or are you thinking, 'I should be enjoying this, it should be fun.' Nobody can force that feeling of enjoying every challenge, and if you don't why should you keep on doing it day after day? My worst nightmare would be to build up a business, sell it and suddenly realise that I have hated every second of the last 20 years of my life, leaving me asking myself why I didn't sell sooner.

Yes, it will be tough, but it will be fun too. It is the sheer nature of entrepreneurs that they will enjoy the gruelling times. They will be able to stay motivated and will love the feeling of controlling their own destiny, even during the tough early days when they're working every hour of the day and living on less than the minimum wage. It is amazing to me how many people fail to realise, as they dream about storming the market with their potentially groundbreaking ideas, that when they launch their business they are likely to go through patches when they will live on virtually nothing. It is almost certain that they will have to take a significant dip in their lifestyle and earnings before they recover.

Enjoy yourself

But when fortunes do pick up, it's the best feeling in the world. I love the everyday cut and thrust of running a business, the deals and the intricacies. They're the fun bit, and they give me a real buzz. It might even be addictive. Isn't it interesting that few entrepreneurs sit back and put up their feet once they've made their millions? There's always a reason to keep going back for more.

'When one door closes, another opens'

It is just too passive in a business setting simply to expect something better to come along. I find that people spend far too much time fixated on the door that has just closed, rather than seeking out all the alternative opportunities available. I am a great believer in the fact that if you are looking for an opportunity you will see it. Which is why, for entrepreneurs, it is less about waiting for the door to open and more about pushing it open themselves or even finding a new way to create the doorway itself.

Chapter 2

What makes a great idea?

I've been a Dragon since the 2006 series, and I have to say that the single aspect I enjoy most, aside from jousting with my fellow Dragons, is seeing the huge range of ideas that are presented to us. As a nation, we Britons are not short of ideas. We've millions of them because we are great inventors. It's almost as if it is in our nature to ask, 'What if I do this? Wouldn't it be wonderful if . . .?' We are all potting-shed entrepreneurs at heart, and I love that.

All the investments I have made in the Den were good ideas that inspired me, and asking me to name a favourite would be like asking parents to choose their favourite child. But to define the type of idea I do like, it is worth mentioning two products that I didn't secure an investment in but that I thought were particularly good: Cuddledry and Nova-Flo.

Cuddledry was the idea of two mothers from Somerset, Polly Marsh and Helen Wooldridge. They hit on the idea of a towel that attaches like an apron after they had been discussing how difficult it is to juggle the task of lifting a slippery and wriggling baby out of the bath and then trying to wrap them in a towel, which may have to be held awkwardly under the chin or even in the teeth.

The pair noticed that many parents had resorted to laying their charges on the bathroom floor while they grabbed a towel, which is obviously an unsatisfactory solution for a baby who has just been plucked out of a warm bath.

Polly and Helen experimented with wrapping teddy bears in torn-up sheets until they came up with the concept of a towel that attaches to the parent and can be removed single-handedly with easy-release poppers. The reason this idea ticks all the right boxes with me is because it is an invention that mimics the way people already behave – or want to behave. It is not an off-the-wall idea, nor is it even a huge step forward, but it came from simply standing and thinking, 'Why isn't there something that does this?' What better starting point for an entrepreneurial venture can there be?

The other idea, Nova-Flo, is a mechanical device that senses the water level in a bath and automatically shuts off the taps if it is in danger of overflowing. The man behind it, James Barnham, is a smart guy who, while he was still at university, decided to tackle a problem that leads to thousands of damaged properties every year when taps are inadvertently left on. Obviously, an electrical solution was a non-starter, so he came up with a simple mechanical bath overflow trigger. It is an excellent example of an innovative, well-packaged and simple solution to a niggling problem.

We Britons may come up with tons of great ideas like this, but sadly millions of them fall by the wayside every year because they

Brilliant ideas are good, but brilliant business propositions are what count

don't get taken any further. The way entrepreneurs make their millions is to turn that brilliant idea into a brilliant business proposition. At the risk of stating the obvious, people who have remarkable ideas but then fail to do something about them are not entrepreneurs; they are simply people who have good ideas. An entrepreneur, on the other hand, makes that idea a reality and then sells it. First stop is a business proposition that says: 'I have had this idea, this is why I am the person to exploit it and this is the way I will go about it.' The next step, quite simply, is to get on with it!

It doesn't have to be new to be exciting

Ideas themselves do not have to be the greatest inventions for years, and in fact they rarely are. Most successful ideas come from tweaking an existing product. Think of the fuss people made about sliced bread. Sometimes the thing to do is refine and improve a product or service that's quite rough around the edges. MP3 players, for example, had been around for a few years before the iPod came along with its sleek, easy-to-use design. Alternatively, there can be opportunities if you strip something back to its bare essentials so that it's a lot cheaper – think easyJet and the revolution in low-cost flying. My point is that entrepreneurs should never be afraid of tackling a market that is already working well; they just need to be sure that they've got an edge.

If a product is to stand a chance in today's competitive environment, at a time when consumers are scrutinising every penny they spend, it needs a unique selling point (USP). A USP is the feature or benefit that gives the consumer enough of a reason to switch from something that already exists to a new version. The new product may be cheaper or smaller; it might have extra functions or simply update a previously standard design with a new range of colours or looks. It doesn't mean that the original wasn't a good idea in the first place; it just has to present consumers with a compelling reason to switch.

In some ways I would actually be quite nervous about a new product if it emerged that there was absolutely nothing like it on the market. I instinctively feel it would be dangerous if there was no competition whatsoever because this might be an indication that there is no market either. I'm not saying that products that create their own market because they are so completely new and unheard of never succeed – they're just really rare. The only example I can think of from my lifetime is the Internet, and that is not so much a product as a whole new means of communication and expression.

My view is that having competition is never a bad thing. It tells you that there is a market out there, and if it is a strong market, all the better. If the competition is doing badly it could mean that they are getting it wrong, in which case here is your opportunity to get it right and grab a share of that market for yourself. Either way, having competition is a really great way to help determine your USP.

As with many other aspects of business, finding your USP is all about asking the right questions. What makes this idea

Give your product an edge and then tell everyone about it

different? Is it offering anything unique? Does the person behind the idea have any special skills or expertise? Is the business focused on a niche segment or on the mass market? Is there anything special about the way we are planning to do business? Answer these questions with complete honesty, and I guarantee a clear picture will emerge.

It is quite possible that the entrepreneur, or even a key employee, will be part of the USP. Perhaps they already have a lot of experience with the product or market or they might have expert knowledge of the manufacturing process. Many successful start-ups have been formed when a highly knowledgeable employee has left a company to make an improved product on their own.

With a product like mixalbum.com, the music download website, the USP was immediately obvious. Mixalbum.com has the only software in the world that can mix dance music together the way it does – it's literally unique, and that's the selling point. Unsurprisingly, it is more difficult to pin down the USP for mainstream products such as telephones or televisions of which there may be hundreds on the market.

It is not impossible, though. Take Weststar, for example, the company that my parents founded when they bought a run-down caravan park on Lizard Point in Cornwall. When I started out at Weststar it was one of 3,000 holiday parks in the UK. I had to think hard about what it was about Weststar that made it so successful. I gathered the senior team around me and asked them too. What is it about Weststar? Why is it so attractive? Why do our customers keeping coming back?

The message that came back immediately and strongly was that all our parks were in very special places. Indeed, it was what the customers had told us again and again: they had had a fantastic holiday and the locations were absolutely amazing. So, our USP was that Weststar had special parks in special places. Once we established that, we only acquired parks in special places because once you know what your USP is, the trick is to package it up and shout about it.

Does it have a market?

In series three of *Dragons' Den* Sheila Nelson and Nick Finister from Bubble House Worm Farming appeared on the programme to tell the Dragons about their plastic wormery, which uses worms to turn food waste into compost. It was a good business and the product worked well, and I had no doubt that it would do fine. So why wasn't I keen? Well, I knew that there are already dozens of wormeries on the market in all different sorts of shapes and sizes.

Sheila and Nick were convinced that their USP was that it was an attractive wormery. Made out of sleek black rubber, it was built to stand out from the crowd. My argument was that they were just not attractive at all, no matter how they were made. Yes, they do a good, practical job, but selling them on a USP of good looks was simply a non-starter. With the best will in the world it is an ugly product that also does something that is identical to other products on the market. I did not invest.

I felt that Sheila and Nick had misjudged the size of the market for 'attractive' wormeries, and this is a problem for a lot of would-be entrepreneurs. I've lost count of the times people have stood in front of me and claimed: 'There are a potential 30 million people who will use this product, and if I could only sell to 2 per cent of them I will make £6 million profit within six months.' Had they asked a more experienced person to sense-check the assumption, they would quickly understand quite how hard it is to gain anything like 2 per cent of such a huge market. It's important to get advice, but not just any advice.

The first step that most would-be entrepreneurs take is to ask family and friends about their idea. Starting up a business is, after all, a life-changing decision, so it's natural to run the idea past the people you care about. The problem is, too much advice and feedback from whatever source can be fatal for a fledgling business.

People who are thinking about a start-up get into the habit of asking questions, and pretty soon they are overwhelmed with the sheer weight of advice they get from all sides. I have seen it happen, and it sends even confident entrepreneurs into a complete tailspin.

Advice is useful, but you must bear in mind where it is coming from and with what authority. Your great-uncle Bob might have a lot to say about your widget idea, but having a lot to say does not automatically qualify him as an expert. Similarly, it's worth thinking about how honest family and friends are really going to be if the idea is poor. As regular viewers of *Dragons' Den* will know, I am not shy about telling anyone anything, but even I sometimes hold back from telling friends what I really think. If I like and respect someone I have known for some time I will water down my reaction. Instead of saying, 'That is such a terrible idea,' I will say, 'Hmm, what an interesting thought. Have you considered trying xyz?' It is easy to see how they might come away with a positive impression and tell others, 'Deborah thought it was a good idea.'

I would advise entrepreneurs to find half a dozen people they respect but with whom they don't have a direct relationship and who don't (as far as they know) have any personal axes to grind. They might like to ask advice from their local store manager, for example, if they have already established a good relationship, or perhaps find a contact at a relevant trade association or even, as I mentioned earlier, get in touch with an established business-person. Lucy Buck's elevator pitch to me took some guts, but she did get a response.

Most people will not mind being asked for advice, and even if they do not have a clue about a particular industry, they will probably have some useful ideas. I would call them up and say, 'Before I go too far down this route, how does the business proposition sound to you?' Then, and this is key, I would listen to their responses and take them on board. Most would-be entre-preneurs get so excited about their idea and want to be in the business so much that they don't really listen to what people are telling them.

What is most important in gathering advice is to ask the right people and not ask too many of them. There has to be a point at which you draw the line and say, 'Thanks very much, I have heard it all and this is what I've decided to do.' I can always spot the people who are not genuine entrepreneurs because they are the ones who go on asking more and more questions. They rely too heavily on other people and somehow can't bring themselves to get to the point where they actually get on with it. They put themselves in a limbo of constantly seeking reassurance. What they are trying to do, I think, is avoid the mistakes that are a product of inexperience.

Naivety, though, is not necessarily a bad thing. It is so refreshing to meet new entrepreneurs because they are not loaded down with preconceptions. An experienced businessperson might say, 'Oh yes, we tried that before and it didn't work.' Inexperienced entrepreneurs don't know what can and can't be done. They don't know what didn't work five years ago or what was shelved as too expensive three years before that, and even if they're told, they might say, 'Hey, so what if it didn't work before? Let's try it this way today.' And, do you know what? They will probably find a way to do it successfully.

Even as a business matures I would always pair an inexperienced person with someone who has been around the block. Inexperience is a great counterbalance. If your business keeps running back to experience it will never actually move forward.

Is the timing right?

The timing of an idea is so important that it can make the difference between surviving and sinking without trace. There is no point in introducing a brand-new product before customers are ready for it, and that is why it is useful for an entrepreneur to get out of the potting shed once in a while and get plugged into the zeitgeist to understand what is making people tick right now. Even an excellent product would struggle if it were launched at the wrong time. I have spoken to countless people who tell me they introduced a concept ten years ago that failed spectacularly, yet today it is hugely successful.

I was at a dinner party recently and another guest was proudly telling me how years ago he came up with the idea of a 'smart fridge', which would automatically reorder groceries. Well, that is fascinating. The fact remains that, despite dogged attempts by many leading manufacturers, no one, including the man I was sitting beside (who hadn't actually done anything about his idea), has so far managed to get a viable product on the market.

When this man first thought of the idea most people were not even used to shopping on the Internet. The idea of a fridge topping itself up from the local supermarket was perhaps too big a leap of the imagination. Now that we are all used to ordering online, manufacturers have not yet overcome the problem of mass-producing smart-fridge technology at a price that most consumers are prepared to pay for such convenience. So the timing still isn't right – it's too early.

But if you leave it too long you may find it swiftly becomes too late. Market research can prove invaluable in determining an idea's potential and to gain some idea of the customer the product or service will attract. But the key is to spend as short a time as possible on this activity. A trip to the library or a few hours online should set you well on the way to understanding the market. Years of painstaking research are not a practical option because by then the market will almost certainly have moved on. If it is a product or service that needs to hit the market now, do the research and get it out there.

One of the main tendencies at this stage is to overcomplicate the whole thing. Sometimes entrepreneurs become so wound up with the minutiae of how they might bring their cherished idea to market that they end up doing nothing. And sometimes they hold back the launch of the product as they try to make sure it's 100 per cent perfect. Do we really want perfection? Of course, we should strive for it, but there are few situations where it is a good thing to wait for it. My view is that in many cases entrepreneurs would be better off getting a product out on the market if it is at least 80 per cent right rather than completely missing the moment by trying to set up everything absolutely perfectly. Perfection may never ever happen. It is easy to lose sight of the simplicity of a business, yet every venture, if you break it down, is pretty uncomplicated.

Another bugbear of mine – if we're talking about overcomplicating things – is making too much of a fuss about confidentiality and patents. Not long ago a young man came up to me in the street with a huge smile and an outstretched hand. Almost immediately he began to tell me how he could not believe his luck that he had run into me because he had a business that he was on the verge of launching and had been racking his brains about getting directly in touch with one of the Dragons. He was pleasant and polite and asked if he might send me details of his company and idea. 'Of course,' I replied, 'please do.' He was clearly delighted.

Then, suddenly, the mood changed. The reason? He demanded that I sign a non-disclosure agreement (NDA) before I was sent those details, and I said no. He was utterly taken aback, said he would not be able to share his idea with me after all, turned on his heel and stormed off.

Many people will find this surprising because the subject of protecting products is a continual refrain in the Den, but I believe people get far too hung up on this sort of thing.

Let's tackle confidentiality first. I receive approaches from around 100 businesses a week, asking me for advice or to invest in them. I am not going to sign a hundred NDAs every week. An entrepreneur can either trust me, value my input and think that I am a good person to get involved in their business, or not discuss it with me. At this stage I have no knowledge, passion or interest in the idea, and whether they talk to me about it is of no consequence to me whatsoever.

I am not in the business of stealing people's ideas, but equally I am not going to spend my life signing NDAs. I will sign an NDA once I know a little bit about the idea and I am interested enough in that business to see more detailed, commercially sensitive information.

If people get so tied in knots over being protective about their business concepts there is a danger that they will never actually get them off the ground because they won't talk to anybody or show them the product. Yet simply discussing the nature of the business with someone or showing rough plans is unlikely to be commercially sensitive. Commercially sensitive information is something that will give a competitor an edge or help somebody else get there first. It would have to be a completely new idea that has never been envisaged or heard of before to fall into that category. The fact is, as we have already discussed, a new venture is far more likely to be a different take on an existing style of business.

In the early stages entrepreneurs should ask themselves whether it truly is a risk to the project if a wider market knew about the product. If, after giving it cool and calm consideration, they believe it might be of use in getting the idea to the next stage they should find someone they trust and talk to them. The people who are going to make the most difference to an entrepreneur's life are not going to be bothered to sign a confidentiality agreement simply to discuss an idea.

Don't get too hung up on confidentiality and patents

I have lost count of the number of times that would-be entrepreneurs turn down the chance to get in front of an important customer. They say that they do not want to talk to a retail giant such as, say, B&Q, because B&Q will just copy them next year and cut them out of the loop. Well, they might. On the other hand, it is B&Q's job to retail goods. They get good ideas and new products brought to them all the time. They are not actually in the business of stealing other people's ideas. It might happen, and I cannot guarantee that it won't, but most retailers would prefer to buy from a supplier than bother setting up the manufacturing processes for one item out of the 50,000 items they stock. Presumably they thought they were all good ideas when they first saw them presented or they wouldn't be stocking them.

Patents are a slightly different matter because they can be crucial to making the business model work. I can think of two of my business investments that illustrate both ends of the patent requirement spectrum rather well.

The first is mixalbum.com, the music download website that appeared in series three. Ian Chamings, who coincidently trained as a patent lawyer before starting up mixalbum.com, had already had a unique patent on the system before he presented it to the Den. He realised he needed to secure the patent because this was a product that didn't exist anywhere else in the world. Now if anybody pops up and says, 'Well, I've been doing that for years', they won't have a case because he's patented the programme.

In mixalbum.com's case the patent is extremely valuable and was vital in securing the investment from myself and Theo Paphitis. Without it, hundreds of other people could do what Ian had done.

The patent implications of Buggyboot, which I invested in in series six, seem to me to be entirely different. The Buggyboot Plus is a wheeled shopping holdall that can be attached to the back of a lightweight buggy or pushchair. It solves a perennial problem for pushchair-users who hang heavy shopping bags on the back of the pram, only for the whole thing to topple over once the child gets out or – worse still – while the child is still in it. When the holdall is not in use, it can be removed, leaving a stand-on platform for older children. There is also the Buggyboot, a bag-only option.

When Charlotte Evans and Carolyn Jarvis pitched the idea in the Den they had already submitted an application for a patent. They were passionate about getting that aspect of the paperwork in order and were a little surprised when I confessed I was not quite as stuck on getting a patent as they were. There are already a number of existing 'buggy board' products on the market. The point about the Buggyboot is it does the job in a better way than the competition. Even if we get that patent, somebody else can – and no doubt will – come in with a slightly different way of doing it. The advantage we have is that we will be getting our product to market first. There is very little point in getting hung up over the patent because there are many other ways of doing the same thing.

I'd say the difference between these two cases is clear. The automated DJ system is an algorithm and is the only way you can achieve that end result. The fact that Ian has the patent says no one else can copy it. With the Buggyboot, on the other hand, it is possible to get the end result in a slightly different way from other products already on the market. A patent would be good to have, but, frankly, it is not the be all and end all. You can only patent the method, not the original idea.

Of course, I am not immune to getting concerned about patents and one occasion does spring to mind where I got really hung up. I often say that one of the Den investments that I have always regretted missing out on was iTeddy. The entrepreneur Imran Hakin had devised a toy that combined the timeless and classic appeal of the teddy bear with up-to-date technology. He called it the iTeddy and it's an interactive teddy bear with a computer in its tummy that is designed to help preschool children learn while they play. He insisted he had a patent and I kept saying, 'You can't have a patent because a computer screen and a teddy already exist.' Indeed, if he did have such a patent he had no business being in the Den because all the world's toymakers would be beating a path to his door.

On reflection, now, I can see that the issue of the patent was neither here nor there. iTeddy was a very, very good product that has since gone on to be enormously successful, securing deals with a number of top high-street stores. I had got so hung up on the patent angle that I stopped considering all the product's other great attributes, and this cost me the investment.

Patents are complicated, and I would simply advise any entrepreneur to get good advice on the subject. If you have something you think is unique and it is an end product, not simply a new way of doing something already on the market, do patent it. But, if you think there could be a thousand ways of achieving that end product, what is the point of patenting? You'll probably get a patent, but so what? Someone else will just make the product in a slightly different way.

Even if the market looks ripe for your product and you're confident yours would be the first of its kind, other factors can intervene and make you think carefully about the timing. Understandably, people have a real fear about starting up new businesses in the middle of an economic downturn. Since late 2007, when the words 'credit crunch' entered the lexicon, borrowed money has become more and more expensive, and this poses a real threat to businesses all over the world. I agree that it is a risky time, particularly for novices, but I also think that it is under circumstances like these that true entrepreneurs really shine.

A really good business will survive in good and bad economic cycles, and I certainly wouldn't argue against going into business during a downturn. When it is more difficult to raise money and find customers it simply means an entrepreneur has to get their proposition finely tuned for the market and leave no margin for error. Being forced to be more rigorous in your approach is not such a bad thing. If entrepreneurs have to get every aspect of the idea and business running properly it will have a better chance of survival. If an idea survives the downturn, wow, is it going to fly when the economic cycle goes up again.

'Don't reinvent the wheel'

Just because an idea isn't completely original doesn't mean it's not worth doing. Entrepreneurs will spend their lives trying to make the wheel just a little bit better. There are times when someone can make a single tweak to improve a product or service and that contribution will suddenly make it soar.

Chapter 3
What makes people invest?

In April 2006, when I first received the call from *Dragons' Den*, I was decidedly underwhelmed. It was only a year since I had completed the £33 million deal to sell most of my stake in Weststar to Phoenix Equity Partners at a considerably higher price than a deal I had turned down in 2003, and I felt I had reached a really good stage in my life. I still owned a 23 per cent share in Weststar (which I sold in 2007, when Phoenix sold Weststar to Parkdean Holidays for £83 million) and had an active role in acquiring new parks that I really enjoyed. I was not prepared to let anything spoil what I had achieved.

I had come to the attention of the producers thanks to widespread stories about the success of the holiday-park industry. There was a real buzz about the sector. Bourne Leisure had snapped up the great British institution Butlins in 2000 and followed their success by buying Warner and Haven, and US investment giant Blackstone had just bought holiday-village operator Center Parcs in a bid worth £265 million. Suddenly the holiday-park industry was well and truly on the investment map.

Dragons' Den, which had lost Rachel Elnaugh from the line-up, was clearly on the lookout for another woman, and I was told that my name kept coming up. The Phoenix deal obviously helped, and I had just been named one of the UK's top 50 female entrepreneurs.

My initial reaction was lukewarm to say the least. I have always been only too well aware that once you put yourself in the media spotlight you can easily lose control over what happens next. I have seen too many people take that first tentative step into the glare of the media before it all goes horribly wrong. Two years later they find they are 100 steps away from where they ever wanted to be, swept along by a relentless appetite for controversy, tragedy and conflict in a generation brought up on reality TV and celebrity tittle-tattle. I was nervous about putting myself into that situation and losing control over the life I had worked so hard to build for myself.

I am naturally curious, though, and I love the buzz of new challenges, so I let the *Den's* producers speak. During the course of two telephone interviews, I became increasingly impressed by the team. The questions they asked were not flimsy, they were tough, searching and to the point – a technique after my own heart.

After my first screen test I was still not convinced that the programme was for me. It was not until the second screen test, which was held alongside Duncan Bannatyne and Richard Farleigh, that I had a sense of just how challenging and fun this could be. Driving back to my home in Somerset after my day in the studio, it suddenly hit me that I would have been extremely disappointed if I was not offered a seat in the Den.

The rest, as they say, is history. In 2006, just days before series three was due to start filming, the call I had been waiting for came through, and I signed up to become a Dragon. I was thrilled.

To coincide with my Den debut I launched a personal website and added a section entitled 'Pitch your Business'. This is an opportunity for entrepreneurs who are seeking an investment to get in touch by sending in a summary of their business proposals. Thanks to the publicity around *Dragons' Den*, I receive on average a hundred approaches a week, and many more around the time the programme is transmitted.

The experience has provided some useful insights into how entrepreneurs tackle getting investment, and I have to say that my conclusions are not generally positive. I often hear start-ups complaining about how difficult it is to secure finance, yet in my experience entrepreneurs rarely give would-be investors enough information to persuade them to part with their hard-earned money. Today, more than ever, an entrepreneur has to present some pretty compelling reasons for an investor to part with their cash, which means presenting a rock-solid pitch as well as some convincing numbers. They could shorten the odds considerably by thinking carefully about how they contact potential investors and what they send by way of introduction. The first – and most obvious – step is to find out who actually makes the investment decisions at a company.

In my case, for example, you won't be surprised to hear that it is not actually me in the first instance. I employ a former commercial manager from Weststar to filter the approaches. A proposal does not get past her if she does not think it represents a good business proposition. It is only after looking at each one in the mountain of proposals that she will present me with the ones she thinks I should consider. I do, occasionally, go through all of the proposals, just to make sure she is picking up the ones that I would be interested in, but I am probably quite unusual in that. In any event, we have worked together for so long that she knows exactly what interests me.

We will sit down together every month, and she will almost act as the pitcher to explain to me why a particular business plan is sitting in front of me and what she thinks it has in its favour. Most investors and private equity houses will employ somebody to filter investment applications. An entrepreneur has to think hard about presenting compelling reasons for their business to get to the next stage of the filtration process and sadly, in my experience, only a handful do.

There's no doubt that it's extremely difficult to get in front of an investor or to raise outside funds, and the credit crunch has made things even tougher. I've said before that I don't believe the economic downturn is a good enough reason on its own to give up on a business, but this is certainly a sensible time for entrepreneurs to examine closely their motives for going into business. If, for example, a business has secured a valuable patent yet the only immediate option for investment is to agree a deal with a business angel, the decision must be carefully weighed up because an angel will often want a considerable stake. If signing with an angel involves giving up 50 per cent of the equity, my advice would be to think about waiting for more buoyant times. If you can wait under these circumstances I would say that you should. The worst reason to accept an investment is because there are no other options. Ignore the cliché that beggars can't be choosers. There are always options for a savvy entrepreneur, it just takes guts and more than a bit of self-belief.

Where there's a plan there's a way

In the face of seemingly insurmountable odds to gain investment business plans are an essential tool and should be written long before you approach anyone for money. Sadly, though, people rarely get them right. They either do not include enough information, or they don't include the right information, or they get so completely carried away that they include everything from where they were born to a detailed essay on how they overcame the odds to build their product.

A business plan should be a simple, step-by-step document, outlining timescales and milestones, what has to be done in the run-up to the launch and what it is all going to cost. The small, niggly details are of no consequence to me, or any other investor, at this stage. What I want is something that outlines in a punchy way what the business is all about, where it is going and what it needs to get there.

I cannot emphasise enough the importance of a well-crafted and concise business plan. This is a vital document, and if it is being used for the purpose of raising funds every effort should be made to present the business efficiently so that an outsider can immediately understand it. You can find a section on all the elements of the perfect business plan at the end of the book.

Writing the plan offers a golden opportunity for entrepreneurs to consider seriously how much they will be paid. Would-be entrepreneurs often say to me, 'It's all right; I'll live on

Business plans should be simple
and concise

£50 a week.' That is just not possible, and few people would come close to living on that amount. People have to understand what their outgoings are and allow themselves enough to meet those outgoings. How focused will anyone be on the business if they are perpetually worried about creditors? Business founders who do not pay themselves enough will waste precious energy getting agitated over how they are going to look after their family and pay the bills. Entrepreneurs have to understand their own personal financial position and build their cash needs into that model.

My philosophy is that if people do well, they should be paid well – as long as the business can afford it. The converse of this is that if a business is going though a sticky patch, the company head should not just stumble along and think, well, I have always taken out X amount a month and will continue to do so. No, if the business cannot afford it, salaries for those at the top have to be cut for a while.

At Weststar I drew a decent salary, supplemented with an annual bonus, which was properly documented and directly related to the performance of the business. If the business did not do well I had not done a good job and did not, therefore, pay myself a bonus. It is well worth writing these payment proposals into the plan.

Sometimes, of course, entrepreneurs will say they have a large amount of money sitting somewhere that they can live on. When this happens I will ask, 'Why are you borrowing to start the business, then?'

This brings me to an important point. A proposition will not be enticing for an investor if an entrepreneur appears to be unwilling to put up their own money. It makes an investor think,

'If this person is not deadly serious about this business, why should I be?' When I bought Weststar, the holiday park started by my parents, I put everything I owned on the line in order to raise the funding. When I did that, it showed the bank I had commitment, which is something every investor demands.

In series four of *Dragons' Den* David Cosgrave and Travis Mcdonough of Orthotic Group Gait presented an impressive device for assessing a patient's biomechanics, which caught many of the Dragons' attention. However, as the pitch went on it emerged that the product had already been launched in an overseas market where it was hugely successful. The pair were on the programme because they wanted £75,000 of our investment in return for a 15 per cent stake in a separate company to launch into a riskier market. The obvious rejoinder was, 'Why would I risk my money in this start-up, when they already had cash to invest themselves from the other business?'

Similarly, in series six toy designer Adam Arber presented his innovative Roadkill range of soft, cuddly toys that appear to have their insides coming out, as though a passing car has squashed them. I'm a supporter of animal charities, so making light of animal deaths in this way wasn't a good hit for me, but also I noticed that one of the current investors in Roadkill already had a large and profitable business. The obvious question was, 'Why don't they invest their cash in Roadkill?' The answer was that they were keen to have a Dragon on board, which I understood and thought was fair enough, but it was still not enough of a reason to encourage me to invest.

All of these issues about funding and payments should be contained in the business plan, which is such an important part of the start-up process that I'm amazed how many people misunderstand the plan, dismissing it as 'just an exercise for the bank'. There is a general impression that once it is done and the objective of raising funds is complete, it will be filed in some dark corner, never to see the light of day again.

I fundamentally disagree with this. In my view, a business plan should be an absolute and continuous indicator of how a business is doing and where it is going. It should act as a permanent reminder to entrepreneurs of the things they said they were going to do, and it should force them to check their actions and results on a regular basis. It should be updated frequently with the latest information, and each time it should be reviewed for its validity. If the original plan was well constructed, with a clear record of the assumptions made, this should not be a big task.

Any business – from a start-up venture to an established company – would benefit from regularly referring to its plan. Quite often it will reveal an obvious change of mind about a key aspect of the strategy, and this is an excellent prompt for a review of future goals because they are clearly different from what was envisaged before. That review may show they were wrong in the original plan, but nevertheless the business is still on track. Most of all, though, a business plan is an ever-present marker for the frequent moments when entrepreneurs think, 'Am I still on track?' If they don't have those markers, how can they tell whether it is all going well? But the plan is not just there to give you something to beat yourself up over. It might actually show you that you have achieved goals faster than you originally thought. Getting that business plan out can be quite motivating.

It certainly was a useful exercise in the case of mixalbum.com. Although from the start of the investment Ian Chamings was absolutely on track in terms of strategic actions, such as developing the technical side of the site, it took some time before the financial side flowed through to meet the targets. The reason for this was because, as agreed, mixalbum.com was going for a big licensing deal and it might take up to two years to find the right one.

Of course, if he had been missing those strategic action points on the plan, we would have thought we had a problem, but he didn't, and we could see everything was going to plan. It was clear that he was very much in control of what he was doing, and Theo and I were happy to sit and wait, because we understood that we had a good guy, he had done everything to plan and was ready for the licensing deal, which duly happened.

Ian Chamings has demonstrated how a business plan can be used effectively, because his action points appear in every monthly report that is sent to Theo and me. He has not just understood the need for a plan, but continues to use it effectively month by month.

Forget the investment you want; think about the investment you need

Once you have your plan, you should have a clear idea of the sort of money you'll be needing – and when. Don't fall into the trap that many entrepreneurs stumble into of looking for outside investment without first considering what you are really after. There are lots of opportunities out there; you just have to be disciplined about your approach. It's worth remembering that banks and the government provide opportunities for entrepreneurs as well as for investors.

The first questions entrepreneurs should ask themselves are: Do I need a loan? Could I make do with an overdraft? How long will I need this extra money for? Remember, no matter what way an investment deal is constructed, getting an investor means giving up equity, and that can mean giving up control, which was not something I was ever keen on.

Typically, the seed money to get a company off the ground comes out of the founder's own pocket. After this, the next port of call for many is to approach friends and family. This type of cash injection could come in the form of a loan or contribution, or it might even be an outright gift. I would, however, immediately add a note of caution here. Financial ties with relatives or friends may seem uncomplicated at first, but they can easily get extremely thorny. It is not always the case that knowing someone well or being related to them is a good basis for running a business. I am not saying that it will not work – indeed, I have spent large parts of my career in a family concern – but I would just urge any entrepreneur to give it careful consideration based on sound business reasons.

Consider, for example, how everyone would react at times of high stress (and there will inevitably be many of those as the business is set up). This sort of thing is a real test of a relationship.

Everybody needs to know exactly what they are doing and be really, really clear about their roles. If it's possible to imagine everyone turning on each other or splintering into factions, this is a group that probably shouldn't go into business together. It would be a shame to ruin a business by picking the wrong people to work with, and it would be criminal to ruin a friendship by going into an ill-fated business.

My acid tests for entrepreneurial partnerships are, 'Does everyone feel able to discuss the really tough questions openly and honestly?' and 'Would everyone involved feel comfortable airing all of the difficult issues that will arise when setting up the business?' Many people do find it difficult to broach tough subjects with loved ones because there is often a family hierarchy and shared history in the way. But, if there is a huge elephant of a problem sitting in the corner, everyone must feel capable of bringing it to the centre of the room and saying, 'What is that, what is it doing here?' People who don't feel able to discuss that elephant with each other should not be in business together.

If you think you've found the right combination of person-alities and have decided to go ahead, my next piece of advice is to be rigorous about deciding the terms of the agreement. There is a temptation to be less formal than with outside investors. Resist it! This less professional approach signals a poor starting point and assumes that friends and families do not deserve the same care and attention that external investors do. Everyone thinks it is easier to take money from friends or family when you are developing a business. I'd say that it is much easier to take it from a third-party investor because the agreement will be far more clearly defined.

If additional cash is still needed, but only for the short term, I would recommend asking for an overdraft. That is, of course, not as easy as it sounds since the credit crunch, and many firms are even finding that the overdraft facilities they do have are being unilaterally withdrawn. According to a Confederation of British Industry survey in February 2009, more than two-thirds of businesses that had tried to get funds had found that availability had worsened, and it was predicted that the situation was only going to get worse. Obviously, it is hard to know what to do when banks are taking such a tough line, but it is more important than ever to work closely with them. If at all possible, I would advise any company to avoid continually pushing an upper overdraft limit because that will alarm financiers and put the firm under intense scrutiny.

If it is not possible to extend an overdraft or if your financial needs exceed the overdraft limit set by the bank as well as your personal funds, and you have decided not to approach your friends and family, there are alternatives. You can either raise money in exchange for partial ownership in the firm from an investor (this is known as equity funding) or you can try to get a loan from the bank. At the start-up stage it is unlikely that you would be looking at a venture capital investor. Private equity houses usually deal in significantly larger businesses, and there are very few that would even consider looking at start-ups. You'd be better off approaching a business angel, although, even then, there is not an unlimited pool of cash. According to some estimates, just a few hundred businesses a year succeed in getting angel investment.

Another option would be to approach a company that operates in a similar sphere and see if they would like to invest. As well as the investment, this would also potentially afford a short route to market.

With the correct product, such as, say, a water filter for disaster areas, it is also well worth contacting non-governmental organisations (NGOs) or well-known philanthropists, such as the Scottish investor Tom Hunter. If they have a particular interest in the area being served, it might be a good fit. And in any event, you're bound to learn something.

It is most likely, however, that an investment will come from a bank, although even they are increasingly raising the bar before granting start-up loans in the face of the tough economic climate.

One further route for raising cash is through small-business grants. There are seemingly hundreds of schemes available from different awarding bodies, such as local councils, the government and the European Commission. I hate to sound like a killjoy, but when I find out that a company that I am considering getting involved with has a plethora of grants, plus a government-backed Small Firms Loan Guarantee, alarm bells start ringing.

In recent years I have watched new business start-ups become absolute grant junkies. Sometimes, of course, there are genuine reasons why innovation will not happen without a grant, but why should a bog-standard, easy-to-understand business, which might simply be improving a service or opening a shop, deserve a cash handout? The whole point about entrepreneurs starting their own businesses is that they should have a proposition that can stand on its own two feet. I would worry that a business that continuously runs back to grants is never going to survive in the real world.

If I come across a business plan that lists three or four grants

I am immediately alarmed that far too much energy has been channelled into filling in lengthy application forms. I would much prefer that the company got on with the task of actually running the business. I would also question whether it would ever be possible to understand the nuts and bolts of the financial aspects if the business is bursting at the seams with grants.

Having said that, I am not, I must confess, completely grant free. I have had one grant in my business career. It was for building an indoor swimming pool for Weststar, in the days when such pools were rare in holiday parks. Weststar is obviously a seasonal business, and although we wanted to install the pool over the quiet winter months we wouldn't have begun to recoup the cost until the following spring. Consequently, we secured a grant from the English Tourist Board. Product development in a start-up or a cutting-edge business can certainly be a good reason to take advantage of grants because the payback period can often be prohibitive without some kind of support. I have never had a grant since, however, and although I understand that they can certainly have their place I would warn any business against being over-reliant on them.

Investors are looking for more than just a good product . . .

Despite being highly entrepreneurial in devising business ideas, many start-ups fail to show that flair when raising money. As I've said before, for the determined investor there are many ways to raise cash, some of them truly original. I am reminded of the inspirational story of Oxford-based Vicky Jewson, who produced her own screenplay, *Lady Godiva*, when she was just 22 years old. Despite receiving rejections from British production companies and being begged by her mother to forget it and go to university, Vicky was determined. She took out a £20,000 bank loan, hired a PR company and a restaurant for the evening and pitched her film idea to 100 wealthy people. TV and radio personality Nicholas Parsons, who had once bought a car from her father, was persuaded to speak at the gathering and told the bemused guests: 'Who knows how this is going to go? But you guys are rich, you are bored, this will be fun.'

Vicky raised most of the £1.4 million that was needed to make the film from seven investors who were there that night, even though none of them was shown a script. She just stood up and sold her dream, and that is about as entrepreneurial as you could ever get. Not surprisingly, perhaps, Vicky is now working on her second movie.

It's a shame that more entrepreneurs don't feel capable of doing this. When entrepreneurs pitch to us Dragons in the Den, I know that it looks like a nerve-racking experience, but if you are prepared and know what you want, there's really not much to it. Just remember, it is not just the business that investors buy into – it's the entrepreneurs themselves.

The key is to know absolutely everything about the business and get that message across in a concise and credible way. I can't stress how important it is to get the pitch right. Entrepreneurs should rehearse the pitch beforehand in front of someone whose opinions they respect, then take their comments on board and rehearse again. If you are not going to use visual aids in the presentation you should memorise the key points so that if you get lost you can easily pick up the thread.

If you have the opportunity I would recommend pitching to the second tier of investment choices first, preferably choosing people who are not going to give you an easy ride. Your pitching technique will improve, and if someone on the 'B list' does offer you the cash you don't have to take it. Entrepreneurs should remember that they are choosing the investor in the same way that the investor is choosing them. They may well come out of the first meeting thinking, 'Hang on a minute, I have something here,' and that gives them a much better story when they go to their first-tier investors. I would advise anyone not to blow their ammunition too soon and get it wrong with their prime investor.

I would begin a pitch by quickly getting an investor's attention with a summary of the business and what it does. Forget the numbers. If an investor does not believe that it does what it says it does they won't believe anything else about the pitch. Convince them that this is a good space to be in. Don't try to be clever by using long words or industry jargon. At best it will baffle the audience; at worst it will turn them off completely.

Throughout the pitch, remember what the investor is looking for. They will want to know what they will get out of it, what their return will be. Pitchers shouldn't just be focusing on what *they* are going to do; they should talk about what *we* are going to do. This is where you are going to get your returns. This might mean an investor's exit, or it might be dividends, or it might be that the entrepreneur plans to buy back the investor's shares over a period of time. An entrepreneur needs to convince an investor that they have thought about the life of the business, about where it is going and its ultimate aim, not just its first years of trading. Investors also like it if the business founder can prove that they are already making headway. For instance, an entrepreneur who says that they want to open a shop does not have as strong a message as one who says, 'I have found a shop in this fabulous position, this is the rent and this is why it is great.'

It is also worth noting that investors will have their own investment rules, and that sometimes means that no matter how good the proposition is, if it goes against those rules there is nothing that can be done to persuade them. For example, in series three Tony Redfearn made a credible pitch for his Chrex Crayfish Farm, but because the proposition went against my personal beliefs I would never have got involved. But just because I don't approve of encouraging the introduction of foreign species into our ecosystem doesn't mean that other would-be investors feel the same.

I don't mind if it's not the slickest pitch in the world, I just like it when I think the person knows what they are talking about. As I have said before, I will often throw in what I call a sidewinder question just to test the depth of their knowledge. It is one thing to learn a pitch off pat, but how does an entrepreneur handle it when I get in behind the detail? I don't want to invest in somebody who is good at pitching; I want to invest in somebody who is good at business. They have to convince me not only that they actually understand their product or service and their market but also that they are the person who should take it into that market. Once I

Only pursue an investment that is right for *you*

believe that, I will believe their numbers. They might have made errors, but they are halfway to convincing me that the rest of their stuff is credible. If they have lost me in the first half, what am I going to look at their numbers for?

I vividly recall the pitch by Ian Helmore in series five of *Dragons' Den*. His Steri Spray company offers a range of showers that prevent legionnaires' disease. It is a fantastically simple idea, which uses ultraviolet light at a low voltage to keep the shower head free of any bacteria before any water flows, which means *legionella* bacteria are killed at the point of exit. I could see straight away that there were a huge number of applications for this product in both the leisure and health sectors, but when Theo Paphitis and I made an offer of £145,000 for a 20 per cent stake in his business Ian's acceptance was delivered in a distinctly underwhelmed tone.

His reaction, following his low-energy pitch, worried me. I firmly believe that an entrepreneur has to be passionate about their product, yet here he was saying, 'All right, that sounds good, I'll accept the offer.' I actually said to him: 'Ian, I'm getting a bit worried now because I think I am more enthusiastic about your product than you are.' I didn't want to drag him kicking and screaming through the whole process, although at the time it looked as if we would get little sign of a reaction whatever we did.

As it happens, I have since found both him and his products absolutely brilliant. He is just one of those people who, when he gets really nervous, counteracts the emotion by becoming over-calm. Following our investment, he has done everything he has said he would, and I occasionally get an email outlining what he has done. I like that. He is a doer. A couple of my investments have been talkers, not doers, and that is not a good combination.

In the real world the pitch for investment should take no more than an hour. Don't get phased if something goes wrong. When Ian Chamings of mixalbum.com made his presentation in the Den he couldn't have got off to a worse start. He switched on the computer, and it didn't work, not a flicker. Given that mixalbum.com is clearly an Internet-based product and that without a working terminal he would be unlikely to pitch his idea, he could easily have fallen apart. He was, however, incredibly calm about the whole thing. It eventually emerged that the fact that the computer was not working was not his fault – BBC technicians had inadvertently switched it off at the floor just before we started filming – but until Ian discovered the cause he engaged with the Dragons, asked them to be patient while he got technical help and carried on in a remarkably collected way. None of the Dragons tutted or got cross because Ian dealt with it in such a professional manner. In his subsequent pitch he explained a complex idea eloquently, outlined why there was a market for mixalbum.com and presented excellent numbers. All in all, it was a brilliant pitch.

Finally, I have two pieces of advice. First, never, ever, utter the words, 'I am the ideas person, not a numbers person.' It is just not good enough to be setting up a business while claiming to know nothing about basic numbers. And it's certainly not good enough to be asking for someone else's money while you're making such claims. You should be on top of what your business is worth, and if you can't even remember that, why should investors trust you to remember what their money is worth? Entrepreneurs only really have to remember a few figures – turnover, profit and cash flow – and they're not difficult to master but are of vital importance. Numbers are a symptom of a business. They show if it is well and healthy or if it's looking ropey. Entrepreneurs do not have to be accountants, but they should know enough to be concerned when the figures look bad and to be motivated when the figures look good.

Of course, there are some people who have genuine problems with the intricacies of finance, and it is all right to rely on the expertise of a financial person from within the company, but instead of saying, 'I am not good with figures,' they should try something like, 'For the detail behind the key numbers, I'd like to pass you over to my colleague, the numbers guru.' That tells a different story.

Not knowing how to deal with numbers can mean that entrepreneurs pay a heavy penalty. When Dr Gili Kucci walked into the Den to present her range of therapies and beauty products for stressed people, the Dragons were immediately impressed. She was attractive, well dressed, smart and charismatic. She appeared to have what it takes. But she fell apart when it came to the numbers, and the pitch turned into a farce with her answer to everything coming out at £55,000. Turnover? £55,000. Net profit? £55,000. She seemed to have no idea, and, as Peter Jones said, that lack of knowledge made her completely uninvestable.

In another instance ex-model Bunny Hargreaves, who came into the Den to pitch for investment for her Crystalboots range of translucent wellington boots with brightly coloured interchangeable socks, tied herself in knots with her numbers. She managed to confuse turnover with profit, and in the end, clearly flustered, she blurted out that we would just have to trust her on the numbers. How could we do that? We had only asked for two

figures, and one of those was wrong, yet she was asking for
£100,000 of our money.

My second piece of advice is never, ever bullshit. Anyone
trying to bullshit or cover up that they simply don't know an
answer to a question immediately alarms me. Someone who
does not know an answer should not try to bluff their way
through. They should say: 'I don't know the answer to that. I
should know the answer, but I'll find out. However, what I can
tell you is this . . .'

I cannot work with people who are not upfront, honest and
straight-talking. An investor has to be able to trust the people they
invest in. They are not there with the entrepreneur every day and
cannot constantly be looking over their shoulders wondering if
they are honest. The more they bullshit, the more they chip away
at that trust.

. . . but if the numbers don't stack up, you won't get what you need

New business valuations are more often than not unrealistic and
overhyped. Time and again I look at a valuation and think, 'Don't
be ridiculous.' Often I can point to half a dozen companies in the
sector, with proven track records, that have done deals at £x, and
yet here is a raw start-up asking for many times that amount. It

would be amusing if it were not so infuriating that my time was being wasted.

This optimism is frequently fuelled by advisers who apply standard valuation formulae, such as the value is six times the earnings. So a turnover of, say, £2 million automatically makes the business 'worth' £12 million. But, valuing a start-up with a catch-all formula is far too simplistic. It is hugely difficult to value any business, particularly a new one, and ultimately it is up to the investor to take their own view based on all the facts in the pitch. They will also discount the price according to whichever factors about the business concern them. There is always something in the proposal that will make an investor feel uncomfortable, and often it's hard for the pitcher to predict what that something will be. Entrepreneurs setting out on this process should ask themselves: 'If I were an outsider, what would worry me about this business? What would I discount it for if it were my money?' The key is to try to get yourself thinking like an investor. Ask yourself: 'What would I pay for this business?'

I would also recommend that entrepreneurs study the business press to get some idea of what companies in their sectors are trading at in terms of multiples of earnings. Look for deals that have been done recently. If a business generating £0.5 million of profit was sold for £3 million, then it is easy to calculate that the company was sold at six times profit. But then it's important to take into account the fact that this was probably an established business with a long trading record and an assured profit. This has to be weighed against a business start-up, which might have no market space whatsoever and be likely to lose money, at least in the short term. On the other hand, a business with low profits but plenty of valuable assets might be valued at a far greater multiplier of profits. As you can see, valuing a business is part science, part instinct, but a significant amount of market and deal knowledge is essential.

When I decided to sell Weststar I held a beauty parade to find the right mergers and acquisitions (M&A) specialist to conduct the sale and called in Deloitte, Livingstone Guarantee and KPMG. I asked them, as part of their pitch, to demonstrate their market knowledge and show me how they would come to a valuation for Weststar.

What they came back with was a table that showed all the transactions that had happened in the holiday-park market over the past few years, the sizes of the businesses sold, how long they had been going, their profits and the sale prices that these businesses achieved. The tables built up a picture of the market and were a helpful indicator of the average price paid.

Valuing a business is never as simple as saying, 'The firms in this sector are all selling on a three times multiple of profits.' Every business is, of course, different. For example, a holiday park with a massive hotel building but producing only £10,000 a year in profits might sell for £500,000 (50 times profits) because the buyer will think they can do a lot more with the site. Meanwhile, something with no assets and producing only profits might achieve a sales price of just three times its profits because it is completely reliant on cash flow and there is nothing underwriting the business.

Supply and demand will affect the price, too. In buoyant times prices shoot up because everybody is looking for investments. In difficult times prices come down because people are more cautious about their investments and simply can't support high prices.

All that the entrepreneur can do is look for market evidence and set the business against the basket of market evidence.

The amount that entrepreneurs ask for their business is, of course, purely personal, but the more homework and preparation they do, the greater the chance of finding the right number and achieving a sale. What they do have to think about carefully is how much of the business they are prepared to give away. It is more difficult to dilute shareholdings or reissue shares later on. Some people refuse to own any less than 51 per cent of a business, whereas others are happy with 25 per cent. It is all very well insisting on retaining 51 per cent of a business, but what if it is not possible to get an investor at that level? Are there other options? Indeed, after the entire process entrepreneurs might well think that they are better off on their own – we've seen it happen in the Den. This is why it is a terribly, terribly personal process.

My preference as an investor in valuing start-ups or early-stage, low-profit businesses is to define what I want out of the business in terms of value in, say, three years, and for a start-up that might be three times my initial investment (or indeed more) if everything goes well. By looking at the cash flow I can work out how much I need to put in and therefore how much equity I need if I am to get my required return on investment. However, if I can see that the numbers aren't going to work for me I'm not afraid to say 'no'.

Moving on from a 'no'

In the long journey of getting a new business off the ground 'no' is a word that entrepreneurs have got to get used to. Many people say that you mustn't take 'no' for an answer, but I would say that that approach will lead to disappointment and frustration. Entrepreneurs may well think that their concept is the best thing since sliced bread, but it is absolutely useless to keep on ramming the point home with an investor who is obviously never going to put their money in the venture. I can't stand it when people stand in front of me repeatedly shouting, 'But it's a great idea!' If they behave in that obstinate way with me, the chances are that they will run their business that way too.

Just getting in front of an investor is an achievement. It would be a pity to waste the experience by being too narrow-minded to benefit from the meeting.

If 'no' is the answer, I would suggest that the entrepreneurs either find a different way of doing things in order to appeal to the investor or go elsewhere. Entrepreneurs shouldn't ever let 'no' stop the dream, but they should realise that the word is trying to tell them something. Indeed, very often 'no' can be a real inspiration. The best entrepreneurs will be told 'no', and instead of hammering away and repeating what they have already pitched they will ask, 'What is it that you need?' They will acknowledge an investor's reticence and use the exercise as an opportunity to find out what it is that is stopping them from investing. That shows that they are tuned in and are willing to adapt to make the business work. A good entrepreneur will be fine-tuning the pitch all the time, and I really like that.

Ask the investor if they are just saying that they have rules that mean that they can't go to more than, say, 20 per cent of the value of a business or if there are other, more serious reasons why they won't invest. The investor won't mind. Indeed, I make it my business to tell people why I am not investing in them. No one learns anything from a bald 'no', which is why I make it clear what is getting in the way of that investment.

In series five, London hair colourist Shaun Pulfrey approached the Den with his Tangle Teezer hairbrush, a small, plastic, kidney-shaped device that uses a three-tier tooth system to help coax difficult, knotted hair into order. Shaun had had two nominations for awards from the hairdressing trade and wanted an investment of £80,000 for 15 per cent of his business to take the Tangle Teezer to the global consumer market.

He was given a rough ride by the Dragons. Peter was surprised to hear that, despite sending out over 300 complimentary Tangle Teezers to the trade and to buyers, Shaun had barely followed up the exercise. Duncan, Theo and James were adamant that it would make no money as a business and indeed James bluntly summed it up as a 'waste of time'. From my point of view, Shaun had immediately got on the wrong side of me by casually mentioning in passing that I colour my hair – which I don't. But, my two main arguments against the Tangle Teezer were that I had something very similar in my stables for grooming my horses, so it simply was not a unique product, and also, because I don't have children, I have no experience of preschool hair-brushing tantrums, so I had no real empathy with the product.

Not having empathy with a product is, of course, not enough of a reason to dismiss a potential investment, but I was having real difficulty finding *my* reason to invest and Shaun was not doing a good job of presenting me with one. Investors are looking for *their* reason to invest and entrepreneurs, if they want to be successful, need to find it.

Having failed to convince us in the Den, Shaun did go on to make Tangle Teezer a very successful product. As well as a thriving Internet sales operation, a number of stores took up the brush. Then, a year after the show, high-street giant Boots agreed to stock Tangle Teezer in 600 of its stores. Shaun took on board a lot of the advice he received in the Den, got his product out to the relevant people, sought feedback and hired a PR machine to ramp up interest. Turnover in 2008 was a respectable £800,000 with an impressive £200,000 profit and projected to rise to a turnover of £1.5 million in 2009.

I am chuffed to bits for Shaun and indeed anyone from the show who goes on to become a success. I know he worked hard on his idea for 15 years, mortgaging his two-bedroom flat in the process.

At the risk of attracting accusations of sour grapes, though, I will say that not all the Den 'rejects' who are subsequently lauded in the press as massive successes are actually quite so successful. I am not including Tangle Teezer as an example, which is clearly profitable, but often media stories of post-Den triumphs do benefit from some scrutiny. If you look carefully at the measure of 'success' it is more often than not based on sales or turnover, and not profit. Now, while it is a great start to be the fastest-selling item in ABC Department Store this year, it means very little if the product is not generating profit. The Den is, after all, about investing in businesses that actually make some money.

'Every day is a new challenge'

Everyone lives through life-changing events and episodes that alter the way they do business or their outlook on life. The point is, however, that they do not happen every day. Every day is not a new challenge, because that would be impossible to sustain. Even if a person is running the most dynamic business in the world, which is absolutely of the moment, there will be days when they just have to get on with the mundane.

I suspect that when people claim that they are fighting off challenges every waking hour of the day they don't actually understand what a challenge is. What they are really talking about are the little issues, such as a customer complaint, an unreliable supplier or a delivery problem – the things that happen to a business every single day – and these are not challenges. These are the engine-room staples that the person at the top either just gets on with or puts processes in place so other people can deal with them effectively. This should not be challenging.

'Challenging' means pushing the boundaries beyond anything that the business has ever experienced before. If entrepreneurs consider absolutely everything a challenge, not only are they wrong, it is also quite likely they will explode with the stress of it all any moment.

Chapter 4

How do you turn your great idea into a great business?

There is nothing more exciting than starting something from nothing. If you are the type of person who is creative and likes to do something different from the norm, running a business will give you the stimulation that you crave. It will be hard work, but there will be plenty of 'yes!' moments as challenges are met and difficulties overcome. It is dangerously exhilarating.

The energy that the experience creates in entrepreneurs is important because they are trying to bring something to life from nothing. But they will gather strength and knowledge by putting themselves out there and learning about things they have never even had to consider before.

In my first business ventures – running a ceramics import business and then a Stefanel clothing franchise – I had to learn about all sorts of unfamiliar corporate processes such as letters of credit, import duties and factoring. I didn't find it daunting. In fact, I had such a thirst for knowledge and a will to succeed that I loved every moment.

It is a feeling that has never gone away. It doesn't matter if I am running my own show, working for someone else or advising an investment, my philosophy is, if you are going to do something, you will get much more pleasure out of it if you really go for it. But, in terms of sheer edge-of-your-seat excitement, there is nothing to beat the start-up phase.

If you can keep your head . . .

In some ways, entrepreneurs are unrealistic people. Because they need to be convinced that they're going to succeed, their projections are almost always overoptimistic. I have lost count of the number of business plans I have seen that say something like, 'I haven't started trading but this is my idea, and in year one we expect to get a 5 per cent share of the market, by year two a 10 per cent share, which means a turnover of £1 million.' In many ways, I like this attitude – it shows a courage of conviction. Indeed, if I saw a plan that said it is going to take ten years to get there I would think: 'Well, what are you bothering for? What is the point of starting a business with negative thoughts, hoping to sell a few products?' In other ways, though, I think it pays to be realistic, and entrepreneurs who get all fired up by their idea should also be prepared for an investor to get out their red pen and knock their business plan back a bit.

As I noted in Chapter 3, when Theo and I met Ian Chamings of mixalbum.com we were not worried that he hadn't yet met the numbers on the business plan, because the licensing deal had not been signed. Apart from the fact he was on track in every other way and had impressed us with his work, we never expected him to reach those numbers. Like all other business plans, it was overoptimistic, and what he really needed was a second plan that said it would take two years longer than he originally thought.

He is not alone. Sarah Lu, the entrepreneur behind youdoo-doll, in which I invested during series five, thought she was going to sell millions, whereas, as I said at the time, because it was a niche product I didn't think there would be a really big market. Max McMurdo at reestore, the man behind 'Ben the Bin', in which I invested in October 2007, was similarly unrealistic.

My view is that the tendency to be unrealistic often begins at the stage when entrepreneurs first begin to pitch for investment. In their naivety, they generally underestimate costs and overestimate income. Everyone thinks that the business is going to take off much more quickly than it does. According to the statistics, nine out of ten entrepreneurs fail because they are undercapitalised. In their inexperience, entrepreneurs don't account for bad payers or for the fact that because they are new traders some suppliers will insist on their cash up front because they have no trading record. A novice entrepreneur will produce a cash-flow projection that says the company is going to sell this many products, that it will receive payment on this date, that holds all suppliers to 28-day payment terms and that within six months things will be absolutely fine. They never allow for the fact that for the first couple of months there will probably not be any income. Day one of a new business is not the day a business starts taking in money. It is the day the outgoings start. Income usually follows much later.

The business plan of every investment I have ever made has been far too optimistic. I always knock the timings back a little bit and remind them to make provision for bad debt. Most business start-ups don't even consider building in provision for any negative issues, but they should because somebody, somewhere down the line, is going to fail to pay on time or even fail to pay at all.

I try to explain to all my investments that the set-up phase of every business venture is rather like having a baby. During this nursery period the business is completely dependent on the founder as its life source, and that person must independently forecast its every need. If the founder does not stay ahead of what the business needs all the time, it will suffer. One day, the business will get to the point where it can stand on its own two feet and toddle on independently, and, like a child who is growing in independence, it will go and help itself if there is no one there to feed it.

It is at this nursery stage that entrepreneurs need to make sure that they can properly provide for the business. A lot of people focus on how they get the business started, but what they should be focusing on is how they get the business to a stage where it is standing on its own feet. These are completely different things.

I often ask my investments, as a test, when is the moment that they foresee that the business will no longer need my support? When is the day they expect the business to be up and running and washing its own face? Most people are not able to answer that. They think in the short term and about what will happen five years down the track, but they fail to account for the years of hard slog between those two points.

Often, after securing an investment in the Den, my invest-ments relax completely and think: 'It's OK now, Deborah will deal with all that!' They suddenly believe that success is assured, and it's not just in the Den that this happens. I have often seen entrepreneurs let down their guard once they secure outside money. They seem to think that money means success, but it doesn't. Success is achieved by the careful application of that money – being clever in choosing what you do with it. Investors will provide money and may even open some doors, but it is the founder of the business who has to fulfil the business plan. The hard work does not stop once an investment is secure, and it certainly does not end once the first product has been built.

The devil is in the detail

At the setting-up stage of a business, perhaps more than at any other moment in the history of a company, entrepreneurs have to know how to look at the bigger picture of getting the business started while simultaneously making sure that no detail is over-looked. I've already mentioned how I think the most important tool at this stage is the business plan, and if you've already put work into this it should help immensely in the next stages.

If you really don't have the flair for detail, then now is the time to bring on board someone who does. When entrepreneurs are looking at a business strategically they need to build a business model that includes somebody taking care of the detail. Somebody has to worry about the little things to stop them turning into big things.

At the foundation of any business are the systems and processes, and the start-up stage is the point at which these are developed. Get them right now, and they will form the lifeblood of your company, steadily working away and making sure everything runs as smoothly as possible. Every business has its own particular set of systems and processes, from ordering and manufacturing to delivery and call logging – the list is endless and individual to each operation. For many entrepreneurs, especially if they are new to a sector or generally inexperienced, setting up such systems can be extremely challenging. I would recommend taking advice from more experienced people and, at first, opting for the safest route possible, even if it's not the cheapest. It's tough enough for a fledgling business without giving yourself extra operational headaches.

Take manufacturing, for example. Companies setting out to manufacture something for the first time with a short initial run should, in my view, start by using a factory that's based in the UK. It will cost more, but because the founders will be able instantly to feel the products and understand the manufacturing process by visiting the factory, they will learn an awful lot. If, for financial or logistical reasons, there is no option but to find a supplier abroad, I would advise finding a good distributor with an excellent track record in this sphere and asking if it is possible to visit the factory with them. I would also want to inspect closely the factory's first ten versions of the product before I gave the go-ahead to make, say, 300,000 of them. The problem with going so far from home is that, even though entrepreneurs may know what their product looks like inside and out, including what it is supposed to do and what it is for, factory managers don't. Even sending a sample out and saying 'That is what it needs to look like' can sometimes not be enough. The product might end up in a different material or with a stuffing that doesn't comply with European safety legislation, or it could even be made in a different colour entirely. The only way to make sure that the design is the same as the one that was originally envisaged is to visit the factory in person so that a sample can be signed off.

Another set-up essential is product delivery. When entrepreneurs are shopping for a courier service, it's likely that one of their primary concerns will be the rates. But, even though the cost is certainly important – particularly to a fledgling operation – it's worth considering factors that are more important than price, so that you do not end up throwing money away on a service that doesn't fit the business's needs. Do products need to be picked up and delivered every day to a set location? Or do they need to be picked up and delivered to various locations around the country or even internationally? Will your customers want to track their deliveries online? All of this needs to be decided before you approach a courier group and discussed openly once you're in negotiations.

The one essential that is most often overlooked in setting up a business, however, is insurance. It is horrifying just how unprepared most start-ups are for the unexpected. Nearly every business I have become involved with through the Den does not have the correct product liability. I ask them: 'If someone cuts themselves on part of a product that you are selling, who will they claim against?' They don't always know the answer, which is that the customer will claim against the shop, and then the shop will claim against the company. I would say product liability insurance is an essential for a small business because it protects it from any liability that arises from damage caused by their products.

Public liability is important too, even if it's not a legal requirement. Public liability insurance protects a company during business activities from any damage caused by, or to, someone completely unconnected with the business. If, for example, a member of the public tripped over some boxes that were left in the street during a delivery from a company, they could sue that business even though they had never once bought a product from them. At Weststar, for example, there could be up to 20,000 people on site at any one time, so what would have happened had someone injured themselves on a paving slab? It might not have been my paving slab, nor one that was even laid during my tenure, but that does not matter because it was my responsibility to look after it and someone could make a claim against me.

It is a legal requirement for anyone employed by the business (including the founder) to be covered by employers' liability insurance, and you might also want to consider key-man insurance, particularly if the business is highly dependent on one person or a few individuals. What would happen if they fell ill or had a serious accident? Key-man insurance buys a company time to address its problems. There are also specialist insurance policies on the market for things like goods in transit and business interruption, which reimburse the company for any loss of earnings. Finally, just as you have insurance for your car and the contents of your home, a company has to make sure that all of its property and vehicles are adequately covered.

Get the business covered

By paying an amount for small-business insurance every month it is possible to protect a company from unpredictable disasters that could prove to be costly if the cover was not in place or was insufficient. The cost of small-business insurance depends on a number of factors, but the most important thing to remember is to provide accurate accounts of the worth of the business and its assets. Overestimating the value of your business may help in the event of a claim, but it will also push up the cost of the premiums.

A little research on the Internet will quickly give you a good idea of the cover available, and you can even get almost instant quotes, but it is worth discussing your needs with a professional insurance company, particularly when you're getting started. Their questions about what type of business it is, how many employees there are, what sort of equipment is used and so on allow them – and you – to build up a good picture of the range of insurance required.

At Weststar we had a low level of insurance claims and an excellent health and safety record, but with 200,000 people going through the doors every year someone is bound to hurt themselves. We worked hard to create a safe environment, but it is impossible to avoid absolutely every mishap. Indeed, the very fact of running a holiday park made us vulnerable because people were in a strange place and doing things they wouldn't normally do. The sorts of claims we got ranged from broken arms caused by tripping over a step to the fallout from someone leaving something in the washing machine that dyed another guest's clothes bright red.

Anyone in business should consider the fact that someone at some time might make a claim against them. Indeed, it is more likely than not that they will have a claim against them, and with compensation claims now running into millions of pounds anything that is not covered would ruin most small businesses.

Insurance, couriers, factories and accounts are systems and processes that are often seen as the 'unglamorous' side of the business, but I think this is a dangerous view. It is these systems that keep the business alive and, when they function properly, allow entrepreneurs to focus their attention on the more creative aspects, the part that will make a company fly. Entrepreneurs should devote time to making sure all the systems work like a well-oiled machine – I think of them as the 'engine room' of the business – and then check on them regularly. I like to build in indicators, such as response times and financial calendars, that will alert me if any core processes are not functioning correctly.

On the financial calendars, for example, our financial close-off at Weststar was always the last Friday of the month, and I established a system by which management accounts would be produced from these figures within 14 days for a board meeting the following week. If this did not happen, it would tell me a lot. For example, if the accounts team couldn't get their numbers together, it might mean that the parks were not providing them, and if the parks were not providing their numbers there was clearly an issue at the parks. These basic systems and processes always tell you a lot more than simply what is going on in your accounts.

If the engine room does not work well entrepreneurs run a real risk of losing control of their business – they will have no idea whether it is working or not, and they will have to resort to relying on luck. I don't like relying on luck. As I have said many times, I like to be in control.

Everything should happen for a reason

So much is happening in the start-up phase that it can be difficult to keep all the balls in the air at once. One bit of advice I would give, however, is to make sure that you always remember why you are doing anything. This should really help you focus on what is truly important. For example, the process of starting up is all about creating an identity for the new business, which is a genuinely critical goal. Yet it is fascinating how many entre-preneurs get distracted when they are striving to achieve this by endless discussions about names, fancy offices and over-elaborate launches. Of course, entrepreneurs should be concerned about the impression their company will make, but spending hours agonising over what they should call it is a waste of time. It makes little difference to most businesses what they are called. It is only important to spend time over a name when it is a retail brand or the trading name of the business, and even then I would not spend hours on this exercise. I have ended up with some really odd company names for my businesses, and it has mattered not one jot.

I don't get hung up on names. All my company names, even Weststar, were bought off the shelf. I was just shown a list of names by my accountant and thought 'That one will do.' In fact, we always meant to change Weststar's name, then one day I realised it did not matter any more because we had created 'brand Weststar', and everyone knew the name and understood what it stood for. It is the same for all brands – even Coca-Cola started out as just a name.

Don't waste a second on selecting a company name. Call it after your cat or your first love, and then forget about it. What is more important is to concentrate on the brand of the business. That is the issue. What you do need is to think of a name that hints to the customer what the brand does. It doesn't have to be 'I am a clothes shop', but it needs to sound like a clothes shop. Then, get a list of alternatives and ask people what they think this company does. Certain words evoke certain emotions. That is really easy research to do.

Far too many entrepreneurs are obsessed about having their name on everything. I have never named anything after Deborah Meaden. It's not a particularly brand-friendly name and frankly, *Dragons' Den* notwithstanding, does not say very much. Now my brand sits in a particular space because of the TV show, but my brand is Deborah Meaden as a Dragon. But just suppose that I started making Deborah Meaden Fluffy Pink Slippers, people would be very confused indeed. They would ask, quite rightly, what is the Deborah Meaden brand that we recognise doing in that particular space? That is the risk people run if they are not

Don't get hung up on
names or status

very clear about what their brand is. They can get out of their space once they have established their brand in a good and solid way, but until then the name has to have a meaning to the customer.

As well as names, I've noticed that new entrepreneurs can get hung up on offices. I've seen many start-ups waste money on a flash office in the centre of town to show they have arrived on the scene. This tendency to 'over office' often comes when a company gets an injection of cash through an investment. Business proposals for investment invariably feature a note that says some of the money will be going towards new offices, and as an investor I will always check whether new offices need to be as much of a priority as the proposals seem to suggest. It is true that there are times when getting a new office will help push a business's boundaries. There are some market segments, after all, where front is quite important: creative agencies, for example, need to be sited in a creative environment. Market Intelligence International, a research company in which I invested, started off in extremely modest offices in King's Cross, London. In the early stages it needed only a small amount of space because it was mainly staffed by homeworkers and the telephone system allowed remote working. However, I could see that there was an opportunity to push the boundaries of the business and encouraged them to move to the Business Design Centre in Islington, which was a more visible and businesslike statement for the company.

I would, however, always question the need to move base. It's costly, after all, and if there is no possibility that clients will visit, why on earth would anyone spend a fortune renting an expensive office suite other than to make themselves feel big and clever? They may say that 'first impressions count', but my own view is that sustained impressions are far more important. After all, how often do you meet someone, feel very impressed for the first five minutes but two hours on realise that actually, though they may be charismatic, they are talking utter nonsense?

Unsurprisingly, I'd recommend a similarly common sense approach to launches too. Should the business be launched with a bang at a glitzy industry party, or would it be more appropriate to go for a more low-key option? I would counsel most businesses against holding a launch party unless there is a very good reason or, possibly, a celebrity connection. Not only is it quite hard to whip up the support and exposure for a party, but by throwing open the doors in such a public way a big launch can make a business a hostage to fortune. If it's not fully operational and efficient on day one it will attract no end of bad publicity. Who doesn't recall BAA's disastrous launch of Heathrow's Terminal 5 in March 2008, when software glitches led to hundreds of flights being cancelled and piles of luggage going missing?

The alternative is to keep the launch low-key – a so-called soft launch. Indeed, if it is a web-based operation or anything where software is involved I would rigorously test it for a few months before opening it up to the public. With a soft launch the business is not exposed to scrutiny until it knows that all the stock is physically there and it has seen the new transactional website actually working.

The beauty of a soft launch is that businesses can be honest with people during this stage. If your systems aren't yet fully operational, you tell your customers that the business is just getting started and is not fully up to speed yet. And you can detail your plans for improvement, hopefully encouraging them to come back. As a new kid on the block, all you need to do is to sound as if you are in control.

Finally, launching a business is quite a daunting moment, but at the same time it is often a bit of an anticlimax. No matter how good the early sales and marketing have been, not many potential customers know the business is there yet, and the phone will not be ringing endlessly with enquiries. Things will inevitably take some time to pick up, and the trick is to keep working through the lulls so that you're ready when things get frantic.

Of course, if it is a retail operation the launch-with-a-bang option is probably the only option. If there is a physical product, together with a fully staffed shop, there is no alternative but to let everyone know straight away that the business is there.

When I launched my Stefanel franchise in Taunton I began my PR campaign by taking over a big nightclub and giving away free prizes all night. The evening and the resulting local publicity gave the store opening a real buzz. Then disaster struck. Just days before our official opening day it emerged that more than 50 per cent of our stock was stuck in the Alps, at Mont Blanc, thanks to an Italian lorry-driver strike. Although we had some stock, it was not enough to open the shop and certainly not enough to match the interest we had created with our PR campaign.

I could have opened with what little stock I had and muddled through, but what would that be saying to my customers who had bought into the notion of this stylish Italian boutique bursting with the latest designs? I wanted to run this business on the basis of zero tolerance to cutting corners and sloppiness, and I wanted to start as I meant to go on. So instead of panicking or falling apart, I got straight on to the phone to the West Country TV news channels, which, as local media always do, were looking for a 'home-grown' angle to the massive strike in Europe. They loved the story of a new fashion store in Taunton being forced to postpone its glitzy launch thanks to the Italian lorry-driver strike. It made a great local-interest piece and generated acres of publicity. When we did eventually open we were flooded with customers who visited the store to find out what all the fuss was about.

When I was starting out, I refused to see things as obstacles, and this ability is never more important than at the launch stage.

Honesty is the best policy

When you move into a new home you naturally assume that everything will work. Turn on the taps and water will flow, flick the switch and the lights will come on, and turn the key and the door will lock. We are used to things working from day one, and it is rare that we find ourselves in the position of having to create something out of nothing. Yet that is the position that entrepreneurs put themselves in. When you're starting a business, nothing happens unless you make it happen and, not only that, you may not even know what is supposed to happen because you are making it up as you go along.

No entrepreneur could, or even should, spend time thinking of absolutely everything that might happen or how they will tackle it if it does happen. They would spend so long thinking about 'what ifs' that they wouldn't have time to do anything else. No matter how much planning you have done, there will always be something that has been overlooked. This need not be a setback. When this happens entrepreneurs simply have to think on their feet, and the truth is that if you are the sort of person who likes the start-up phase, dealing with the unexpected is the best bit. You will thrive on problem-solving because it is the stuff that gets the adrenalin going.

But, while the start-up adrenalin is flowing and solving problems it is also important to be honest with yourself. Again and again I see entrepreneurs who feel that they need to appear positive and who use this as a reason for not being truthful with themselves or with their would-be investors. People find it difficult to tell me, as an investor, about something bad and that destroys the all-important feeling of trust. Often, when they do summon up the courage to tell me some bad news, it is too late to do anything constructive to resolve it. After months of cheerfully saying everything is fine, there is always a point when bad news can no longer be hidden because it becomes blindingly obvious. So suddenly I get absolutely devastating news and am left thinking: 'Hold on a minute – where did that come from? Last week this company was telling me that everything was brilliant.'

If there is a serious conversation to be had with an investor, my top piece of advice is: have it immediately and never, ever do it by email. Emails are for simple, direct stuff and should be kept strictly to non-conversational items, such as last week's sales figures and key performance figures. If you are 'discussing' important operational details by email, neither party is properly listening to the information or gauging each other's reaction. Many people use email as a way of protecting themselves from having a difficult face-to-face conversation. My argument would be that this is exactly what email is not for. If it gets to the stage where you are deliberately hiding behind technology you should definitely be picking up the phone.

I make it clear to all my investments that I expect them to talk to me direct if there is a problem. If something is not right, pick up the phone, set out what is wrong and let's find a way to fix it. Don't just fire off a series of emails and feel relieved that the problem has been deferred for a few hours. Pick up the telephone and outline the issue, by all means sending background information in an email, but communicate rather than correspond.

There is also an element of time management in here. Entrepreneurs keep telling me how busy they are, but they will sometimes spend 20 minutes composing a lengthy email when they could have dealt with the issue over the phone in less than five minutes.

As soon as I have agreed to invest in a project I always hold a meeting with all the key players involved to discuss the aims of the business and its strategic goals. I need to make sure that we all have a common purpose. It would be awful if I put my money in and then some way down the track someone pops up and says, for example, 'I don't think we should have shops in the capital,' and I am left thinking, 'Hold on, that is what I thought we were doing.' As an investor, I want everyone to get the processes right, to understand what they are doing and to have thrashed out the various combinations of 'What happens if . . . ?' questions. In fact,

I often insist on this information being set down in writing in a well-considered shareholders' agreement.

The truth is that with every start-up business something surprising will happen. It might be a good surprise or a bad surprise, but when the bad stuff happens the surest way to fall out is if there is no agreement on how it will be handled. Once the agreement has been signed, ideally it can be put away and never referred to again. But, if things do go wrong, it makes things a lot clearer if everyone's intentions are there in writing. If not, you might find that accusations start to fly and nobody ever admits it was their fault. The entrepreneur will blame the investor for not providing more money when it was needed. The investor, in turn, will blame the entrepreneur, saying the business was clearly already in trouble, so why would they pour money into a failing venture.

The best thing you can do to protect your business, as well as putting the agreements in writing, is to communicate effectively from the start. Be honest and realistic. Your investors haven't simply lent you money; they own part of the business and will want to help you get it back on track. And it's just common sense that if you can spot a problem early, you're more likely to be able to nip it in the bud.

Investing in entrepreneurial businesses can be risky, but I have always accepted that I am in a high-risk environment. Since starting as a Dragon I have had just one failure among my investments, JPM Eco Logistics, the environmentally friendly haulage company, which went into administration in January 2009, just as the recession really began to bite. It is a blow, but that is the nature of what I do. As long as I get more investments that are successes than are failures I have done my job.

'360-degree thinking'

The phrase '360-degree thinking' should be put away in a locked box along with 'blue-sky thinking', 'thinking out of the box' and countless other meaningless phrases that imply that otherwise one-dimensional, dull, uncreative thinking is the norm. Businessmen who pepper their language with these wretched clichés are just saying that they don't have an original thought and they don't have a good command of the English language either. Any business discipline requires creative thought, but creative thinking should be an everyday occurrence not simply trotted out when demanded and on special occasions.

Chapter 5

What about buying a business or running a franchise?

If you dream of being your own boss but haven't yet come up with an amazing idea for a start-up you might think about buying an existing business. I often think that just as much, if not more, entrepreneurial skill goes into turning around an existing business than it does in starting up a new one. It takes the vision to spot a business that has potential or is doing well in spite of itself and the nous to see the improvements you can make.

I remember the day in 1988 when my parents, Brian and Sonia, asked me to head to the Lizard Peninsula on the southernmost tip of the Cornish coast to 'take a look' at a caravan site they had spotted. Before that, they had already set up, bought and sold several businesses together and grown increasingly affluent and successful throughout my childhood. I did work briefly for the family firm shortly after leaving Brighton Technical College, but I quickly realised that, in their eyes, I had not graduated from the little girl who kept forgetting to pick up her toys and tidy her room. In consequence, I had gone off to do my own thing. However, as families often do, they still used me as a sounding board for new business ideas. Therefore, on that uninviting, grey, winter'sday, I found myself crawling along the A30. The freezing winter rain was lashing my car almost horizontally. Although the area is undeniably beautiful and rugged, with the rocks and cliffs of the coastline punctuated by tiny harbours studded with small, whitewashed fishermen's cottages, I confess I was not terribly keen to be there that day. In fact, when I had first checked the map my initial thought was: 'They must be bonkers!'

The proposed site was on the very tip of the Lizard, and you could not get further away from anything in the rest of the country if you tried. The caravan park itself was pretty unappealing, with rows of ageing caravans, an outside pool complete with cracked tiles and peeling paint and a faded clubroom. As I arrived at the reception, which was housed in a Portakabin, I thought that most people's first impressions could not have been worse.

But I could quickly see that, with amazing foresight, my parents had seen beyond the run-down site. It is not for nothing that it is designated an Area of Outstanding Natural Beauty, and even in the depths of winter the views are breathtaking. This remote area offers everything that families yearn for in a traditional English seaside holiday, with sandy beaches and coastal walks, and, of course, the point about a holiday is that you get as far away from regular life as possible.

My parents have always been amazing visionaries and clearly enjoy the energy and buzz of setting up and buying businesses. Even now they are still buying businesses and constantly coming up with new ideas. They typify the true entrepreneurial spirit of wanting to make products work more efficiently or of finding a way to offer a service that is better than anything else on the market. It was immediately clear to them that the team at the park were demotivated because of lack of attention, but they genuinely cared about the holidays they were providing and were really first class. It was truly rewarding to watch them flourish once they realised we were going to invest money and help them make Mullion the very special park it could be.

After buying that site, my parents and the existing team set about transforming it into a top-class holiday park through systematic investment and improvements, adding facilities, a restaurant, bars, bowling and a large entertainment complex. It was that vision that changed the fortunes of Mullion Holliday Park, which is still visited by thousands of families every year, creating new dreams and memories. Who knows, the experience may even help to inspire the next generation of visionaries.

There are lots of good reasons for buying an existing business. It's often a much more straightforward proposition than starting one from scratch. If the business is already doing relatively well, it will be much easier to secure finance to buy it. A proven customer base is a huge bonus, to both investors and banks, and it can even be a comfort to entrepreneurs who are injecting their own cash.

As we have already seen, many start-ups fail because they are undercapitalised. Sometimes the entrepreneurs misjudge how much money they actually need, other times they are simply unable to raise enough because investors are unwilling to get involved in such a risky venture. But, depending on its cash flow and assets, for those who buy a business it is quite possible to borrow a reasonable proportion of the acquisition cost, although it is increasingly difficult in the tough economic climate.

Taking over a profitable business often means that the buyer will be able to take a decent salary from day one, whereas a start-up entrepreneur may often have to wait months or even years to get a decent salary. In addition, in buying a business the acquirer will also gain other valuable assets, such as employees, suppliers, systems and credibility among consumers, which have all been secured by the previous owners. These elements, so essential to a successful business, are hard work to set up from scratch.

It is, however, not all plain sailing. For a start, even though funding may be easier to access, the initial purchase cost of an established business is usually considerably greater than the cost of starting up. The actual process can be quite expensive, too, because the acquirer has to consider building in the fees of accountants, lawyers, valuation specialists and other experts. Entrepreneurs need to make sure they enter into the purchase with their eyes open and their brain switched on.

What's in it for you?

It is astounding how many people seem to go into business for completely the wrong reasons. Having a passion for cooking, for example, is not a good enough reason to become a restaurant owner. Running a restaurant is a complicated job that involves dealing with staff and negotiating with suppliers as well as looking after customers. People who imagine they will be able to spend all day cooking are, I'm afraid, kidding themselves.

The key to buying somebody else's business is knowing that it can do better and being able to identify clearly what changes need to be made, how long it will take, how much it will cost and – most importantly – how much profit those changes are going to generate. Having a clear plan of what it is that can be done to make it better, rather than a vague notion of fancying giving it a go, is essential. The process of due diligence should help you put this plan together because it will help you understand exactly what it is that is being bought. It would be disastrous if, in buying a £50,000 business, you somehow failed to overlook a £500,000 liability. Similarly, another thing to be cautious about is picking up a business that seems to be going for a song. There is nothing for nothing in this world. If it looks too good to be true, then it is likely that you have missed some problem or you are not being presented with the full facts.

Due diligence may seem to be a technical corporate term, but it is actually quite straightforward. It is simply the process by which the buyer makes sure that they fully understand the shape the business is in. The thought process is no different from that for buying anything from a china mug to a family house. Due diligence is something we all do all day every day. We find information about a product, and we make judgements based on that information. Is it fit for purpose? How much does it cost? Is it worth the price that I am being asked to pay for it? When you're buying a business, there is, of course, a lot more complex information to understand, but that, in its simplest terms, is what due diligence is.

The process should, for example, reveal any problems about the reputation of a business. If it is an existing brand that has been performing badly – hence the sale – is it damaged beyond repair? Just how badly has it been damaged? What will it take to fix it and how much will it cost? Of course, a new buyer has a great opportunity to say, 'I have acquired the business and everything will be different,' but they also need to consider that recovery will take time and that, in turn, will cost money. Sometimes brands can simply have had their day, so a good understanding of how customers view the brand and how that fits in with current and future trends will help prospective buyers consider the true opportunity.

Once the research has been done and the plan is formulated, the final question to ask yourself is: 'Will my business model be an improvement on the current plan?' There has got to be a clear reason why you would buy a business. Even as an investor, I always question my own motives for getting involved with a business to see if I would add any value. I am not satisfied unless I believe I know a lot about the area or have identified someone I can bring in who has a great set of relevant contacts and could without a doubt do a better job than the people currently in the boardroom. Having the right skills and expertise to bring the company up to strength is essential. There is no point buying a business that is doing well and is probably at the height of its success with nowhere to go but down. That is just not entrepreneurial.

Get the facts fast and
keep the pace up

If your mind is made up, it is important to keep the negotiations moving on at a respectable pace. Time does kill deals. That does not mean that the entire thing has to be done and dusted in three weeks flat. But, once a timescale has been agreed between buyer and seller, there is a momentum and a moment for this deal to happen. Once it is gone, it is difficult to reignite the initial enthusiasm.

In series five of *Dragons' Den* Peter Jones and I made a £100,000 offer to invest in Cush'n Shade, a foldaway screen that acts as a cushion and a shade for someone who is sunbathing. Initially, I had been really excited about the product and the people behind the business, but, after filming was over, there were delays on both sides when it came to getting the deal done. In fact, by the time we got close to finalising the deal, I had completely lost my enthusiasm for the business because the process had lost momentum, and the investment did not go ahead. Every deal has its moment.

It is not just enthusiasm that can wither. Delays cause problems. Information that has already been supplied becomes out of date, and then you need to see the latest versions, causing more delays. If the business is still trading everyone should be concerned about the lack of focus by the management team and the possible demotivation of the workforce while they sit in limbo awaiting the outcome of the deal. Real-life situations pop up and cut across the agreed arrangements, important decisions become urgent and so on and so on. When I undertook the management buyout of Weststar in 2000, after months of negotiation with my parents, the bank that was then funding the business turned me down. The local branch supported the deal because they knew me well and had worked with me for years, but they were let down by the bank's head office, which had to sign off the agreement and had a strict and unyielding set of investment criteria. I never, not for a moment, thought that meant I was not going to buy the business. I didn't even pause for breath before changing banks, securing the finance and getting on with running the business. My former bank was hugely disappointed. It really didn't think that I would do it. I, however, knew that it was a good business proposition, and a good business proposition will always be able to raise money.

Buying a business can be an emotionally charged experience. However, even if you have dreamed of this moment all your life, I would urge you to try to remain rational. Being passionate about business is important, but if you can't find the right business, or it's not the right time, or something just does not feel right, you should walk away because you might later regret rushing into something. Before you become too emotionally involved, my advice is to keep a cool head and take a long, hard, critical look at the proposition in front of you and then, if you are still totally convinced of the opportunity, get passionate and go for it.

Turning things around

When you take over a business the first step is to identify its strengths and weaknesses. All businesses, no matter how badly they have been run in the past, will have some good qualities that customers liked. The trick is to find them – and fast. The best place to start is to talk to the people who already work there. When you

Identify the strengths – and build on them

meet the team at an acquisition, it is often possible to get a refreshing insight into the company. I always have a round-table meeting with all of the key people in the business at the earliest opportunity and ask everyone in the room: 'Right, what is the plan? What could you do for this business?'

I went through just this process when Weststar bought the Sandford holiday park in Poole, Dorset. Sandford was quite different from the holiday parks that we ran at that stage, and it was important to establish early on which people in the existing team would be comfortable in the new environment and which ones wouldn't.

It was absolutely not a family holiday park: children were definitely tolerated rather than welcomed, and the customer profile was a lot older, which was reflected in the entertainment. There was, for instance, a classic Christie organ in the clubhouse, which used to rise up out of the ground, but it was used only about once a week. However, in due reverence to this event there was no bar in the clubhouse lest the sound of the till interrupted the music of this great beast.

The holiday park was run on an astonishingly hierarchical basis. There were, for example, three parking spaces, in prime positions, reserved for the owners, and an entire table in the best spot in the clubhouse was kept permanently roped off in case the owners dropped in. Weststar wanted to modernise this environment completely by, among other things, updating the clubhouse and entertainments and getting rid of the preferential places for management. The best places in the park should, of course, be at the disposal of paying guests.

Meeting with the team on a one-to-one basis quickly made it obvious who would thrive under the new regime and who would never get to grips with it. The manager of the clubroom, for example, was clearly attached to the old order. Despite solemnly agreeing to instigate the building of a much-needed bar, he stalled and pontificated for weeks and it was obvious he had no intention of getting started because he clearly did not approve. I'm not the type of manager who orders people to do what I say. I like to work with people, but every now and again, if I think that someone is just being awkward, I have to put my foot down. I eventually had to install another general manager in the clubhouse to get the bar built and move the original manager to other duties.

But, just as there are those who will not accept a new way of doing things, there are as many who will surprise a new owner by welcoming a change at the top. Don't forget, it can be frustrating for clever people to watch someone in a senior position destroying a company from within with ill-thought-out decisions. I have often been in businesses where, if encouraged, people at all kinds of level will suddenly offer their thoughts on what actually needs to be done to run the company effectively.

At Sandford, for example, there was a catering manager, called Richard, who hadn't fitted in very well with the old regime. He was a young man, and it was soon obvious that he did not have the same values as the previous stiflingly hierarchical structure. Sure enough, the minute he was given a chance to shine, he did. When I sat down with him and asked what he thought he could bring to the business that he hadn't so far been allowed to bring, he was brimming with ideas. When I watched him in meetings he immediately stood out because he demonstrated the ability to look across departments. Generally, at these sorts of meetings, individual departments are not in the slightest bit interested in what anyone else is doing. Maintenance departments are notorious for it. Yet Richard, quite naturally, wanted to know the effect his catering operation was having on the other parts of the park. He understood that if he could work with reception, they would get more people over to the restaurant for him, or if he could do some deals with the entertainment manager they could work together on a special promotion. In the previous regime this sort of thing was slapped down with the comment, 'You are the catering manager, look after the catering department.' We wanted to hear ideas like this, and meeting someone like Richard in a team is always a refreshing moment.

Being on the inside, he was well placed to offer insights not only into where the company was going wrong but also into what was working really well. Having an honest discussion with an existing team is an easy process to get going. Just let everyone know that they cannot offend you. After all, as a new owner you have no history with them and the past issues of the business are nothing to do with you. I would add one note of caution though: I would be wary of a culture that blames everything on the previous owners, because this will often disguise the real issues.

If their side of the business was not working, I would ask the team members what would they do about it. If the plan sounded credible, I would give them a chance, allowing them, say, six months to prove themselves. They knew the business well and should have a good idea of what would make it successful.

I clearly remember being in advanced negotiations to buy a leisure company when I conducted just such a discussion with members of the senior team. The owner and chairman were not present, and, after an initial period of reticence, the boardroom suddenly erupted with ideas of what they thought the company should be doing and zoomed in on the areas that the company was not focusing on but which they felt they should. This was their moment to say where, in their wildest dreams, they thought this business could be in five years' time. They had some amazing dreams too. It was an inspirational session, and I was really impressed with the team, but unfortunately, though, this investment did not go the distance.

Of course, the new owner of a business must take into account the fact that everyone is apprehensive when a business changes hands. It means a new set-up, and 'new' can mean different and uncertain to some people. They have no track record with the new owner and will be understandably nervous at having to prove themselves all over again. In this sort of environment, with everyone panicking about their jobs, the business runs a real risk of losing its most talented people in the rush to the door. After all, if everyone is sending out CVs, the best employees are clearly going to be snapped up immediately. If these key people leave, the business will lose an important part of its fundamental character, making the task of relaunching it successfully even harder.

There is a short window to get hold of the business and stop this from happening. The only way to react fast enough is to have done your homework thoroughly before signing on the dotted line and buying the business. If the due diligence is done properly, it won't even have been necessary to have met these key people to

Give the key people a reason to stay

know who they are. They are the ones who are behind the departments that are working really well.

Once the key people have been identified, I would immediately let them know that you think that they are good. Be completely honest with them. Ask them to work with you to turn the business around. If they're considering handing in their notice, ask them to give you three months, because at the end of that time they and the business could be sitting on the best opportunity ever. True, at the end of the process, neither party may want to work with the other, but if they don't give the new owners and themselves time they will never know what could have been.

This is exactly what happened with Richard, the catering manager at Sandford. I knew he was good and could get a job anywhere in the country. I didn't plead with him to stay, but after asking him what he thought should happen, I promised to consider what he said and then, if we could commit to it, we would. But, I added, I needed him to commit to Weststar too. Then, and this is important, once both parties have committed to the change, those changes must be made. Actions have to follow; otherwise it is just words.

If there is bad news to give to some employees, I would deliver it as soon as possible. People always expect job cuts as a part of a takeover, and it is not fair to put it off or drip-feed it into the company over a period of weeks. Deliver it, deliver it all at once and then say, that is it, over and done with. As a new owner, you should explain that you have done what has to be done for the sake of the business and the major structural job cuts are now complete. Then the team will no longer have to look over their shoulders all the time, wondering if it is going to be them next week.

It would be a mistake to overestimate how much difference a change of ownership will make to customers. On the whole, customers could not give a fig who owns a business and generally don't find out who does until the day they get upset with the company and decide to make a complaint. Indeed, if customers are not intimately involved with the business on a day-to-day basis it may not even be necessary to tell them about the acquisition at all. Informing customers of a change of ownership will cause them to ask how it will affect them. Unless you can tell them that it will affect them for the better, keeping it low-key may be the best option.

If there is a case for communicating the change to customers – perhaps because the reputation of the brand had been damaged under the previous owners – I would make sure that the problems were well on the way to being fixed or that I had at least seen something happen that would signal change before I announced that it was 'under new ownership'. It is dangerous to make a big song and dance about being the new owner when customers might see nothing new happening for months and months. If people are told that things are going to get better, then boy, they have got to get better and fast. Possibly the best strategy is to run the business for a period to test all the new systems and then choose a moment to tell customers what is going on. Then, if you announce that the company has changed, this will be backed up by your customers' experience.

Buying a franchise

When I was 21 years old, after spending a considerable time in Italy setting up my ceramics import business, my thoughts began to turn to Italian fashion. The brands that caught my eye were Benetton and Stefanel. While the two were on a par in their domestic market and had a huge brand profile, Benetton was far better known in the UK, and I could see that there might be a real opportunity to showcase Stefanel at home. I had a conversation with Anthony, a good friend in Taunton who owned a vacant store, and the idea for a Stefanel franchise began to take shape in my mind.

As if by coincidence, on my next trip back to London from Italy I came across a new Stefanel shop in Knightsbridge. I went straight in and asked where their UK head office was located. Fortunately, their HQ just happened to be in the basement of that particular shop. I asked if they were considering franchising the brand and was told that they were just at the early stages of setting up a franchise operation.

Never one to let the grass grow under my feet, I went straight downstairs to introduce myself to the managing director, who seemed only slightly bemused by this energetic young blonde who had crashed into his office without an appointment. I explained my history, admitted that I had no experience whatsoever in fashion retailing but said that I was already running an Italian import business and had a fantastic shop in Taunton's most exclusive street, Bath Place. Would he, I asked, consider me for a franchise?

As an established brand in Italy, Stefanel was careful about the partners they chose to expand their UK chain of stores. But, after listening to my pitch, the managing director travelled to Somerset to see the shop and agreed to sign us up as franchisees. My franchise for Stefanel, in partnership with Anthony, was one of the first in the UK. Indeed, it was so early in the operation that the company did not even have a franchise brand package. With no guide as to what a shop, or its signage, should look like, we actually ended up commissioning designs ourselves before getting them approved by Stefanel.

Buying a franchise is a useful learning experience for people who have never run a business before. They can cut their teeth with the help of an experienced operator who will already have produced a set of guidelines leading them through the process. It's also lower risk than starting up on your own. According to the NatWest/BFA Survey of Franchising in 2007, 93 per cent of all franchises were profitable after two years, compared to the four out of five non-franchise businesses that fail within two years. But, remember, lower risk also means lower rewards. Entrepreneurs may end up feeling as if they are riding on someone else's coat-tails. It is, however, an option for people who want to be in business but who are not currently in the position to take the type of risk that a complete start-up would entail. Just as I did with my early Stefanel franchise, entrepreneurs might like to use the experience they gain running a franchise for a few years towards a later, independent, business start-up.

When you are choosing a franchise operation, I would recommend that you pick one that best reflects your interests. Like any other business start-up, people are more likely to put the extra time and effort into something they have a passion for.

The British Franchise Association (BFA) holds regular

exhibitions across the UK allowing potential franchisees to check out franchisors and at the same time get valuable expert advice from banks, accountants and law firms. There are also free seminars run by the BFA about becoming a franchisee. Prepare well in advance before attending a franchise exhibition. Go along with a list of franchisors that sound interesting and appropriate questions to ask them. Keep a cool head and resist the urge to sign up then and there. As with any other business opportunity, an entrepreneur should do rigorous due diligence. It is, after all, in an exhibitor's best interest to paint a rosy picture about their business on the day.

During due diligence I would look very closely at the record of a potential franchisor and talk to people in the same industry to gauge their reaction to the business. The franchisor will probably provide names of existing franchisees, who will be happy to give a glowing report. I would not take this at face value. It is important to get a full list of all their franchisees and choose a random selection to contact independently. I would be wary of a franchise operation that seems to be interested only in collecting initial fees from sign-ups and then shows no clear track record of supporting them after that.

If you want your franchise to be successful you will be dependent, to a large extent, on your franchisor, and I would advise anyone to take their time making sure that they get on well and will be able to work with them. It can be hard to extricate yourself from a franchising arrangement if you're not making the income you expected, not getting the support they promised, or if you feel the training is lacking. The moment you feel it may be going awry, you should tackle the problem head-on by contacting the franchisor. I would always stay in touch with the other franchises you approached at the due diligence stage and return to them to find out if they have similar concerns about the way things are going.

If the worst-case scenario happens and the franchisor goes into administration, it doesn't necessarily mean you will go bust too. It will be a stressful and trying time, but there are precedents where franchisees have got together and bought outlets from the receiver. Many franchisees have successfully survived their franchisor going bust by continuing to trade as before, often with existing suppliers and customers.

Personally I have never been a huge fan of the franchise model, because I have always wanted to be utterly in control of my own destiny and I don't like the constraints that franchising brings or the fact that, as a franchisee, you're making a lot of money for someone else. I speak from experience. Aside from Stefanel, the first business that I ran after returning to work for my parents was a franchise operation. By this time Brian and Sonia owned eight amusement franchises on Haven Holiday sites and one holiday park, Mullion in Cornwall. They wanted me to run the amusement-centre side of things, and my sister Gail to run Mullion. After reviewing the business, my reaction was to sell the amusement franchises while they still had some value in them. It was clear to me that we were not far off the moment when Haven Holidays would say: 'Why don't we do this ourselves?'

Buying a franchise is a great way to fast-track into a business, but, like all entrepreneurial ventures, it should be entered into with a clear, cool and business-like head. It is not the easy option, but, in the right circumstances, it is a great way to get the experience you need to run your own business.

'If it ain't broke, don't fix it'

A new business should be constantly looking to move things forward and considering what might be around the corner. Expressions like 'if it ain't broke, don't fix it' are just too passive. Surely the appropriate strategy is to keep ahead of events? A company cannot simply wait for things to happen to the business and then react when it is very often too late to do anything about it.

Chapter 6
Running the show

After selling my Stefanel franchise in 1981, I took on a prize bingo concession at Butlins in Minehead, Somerset. I saw it as a staging post and a great place to make some good money while I thought about what I was going to do next. In the end I stayed for three years and can honestly say it was the most valuable thing I have ever done. Despite all my subsequent years in business, I learned the most about how to set up and run a business from my time at this lively West Country seaside holiday centre.

Bingo is an absolute lesson in business ergonomics. As an operator you have to turn games over, because the more quickly the customers finish a game, the more quickly they have to put the next 20p in the slot to play another round. However, if you rattle through the numbers too fast, you will lose your audience. The only answer is to be constantly tuned into the customers and continually adjust the speed. If you can see a lady in the corner getting flustered, you are going too fast. If the players start to gossip between numbers, you are going too slowly, and going too slowly means losing money. Going too fast might make the players get dispirited and walk away. As the operator and bingo caller you even have a grandstand view to witness, step by step, the moment your valuable, yet utterly fed-up, customer leaves. It is a seriously salutary lesson.

Keep your eye on the clock . . .

I was a good bingo caller, but while I was at Butlins I wouldn't use calling nicknames ahead of numbers such as 'clickety-click' for 66 or 'legs eleven' for 11. Saying clickety-click or legs eleven simply takes up too much time. If I used just the bare numbers I could turn over a game a minute, making £10 a time. If I dropped that rate by 30 seconds by adding the nicknames for the numbers, I would be costing myself 50 per cent of my possible available revenue. It didn't bother my players, who only expect what they get from you. My concession was the only prize bingo on offer at that Butlins holiday centre, and we got people in who had never played bingo in their lives before. I gave them full value for money, it got their adrenalin going, and everyone had a good time. Who needs clickety-click?

An entrepreneur needs to identify early on what it is about their business that really matters. Forget about who has the parking space nearest the front door or which secretary uses too many Post-it notes. What is it that actually makes a significant contribution to the effective running of the business? Entrepreneurs should write it down and keep it as a master list to refer to if there is ever a moment when the 'challenges' seem to be getting out of hand. Good time management is the key to getting everything in the business into perspective.

Know what to spend your time on and when to spend it

Every business has key indicators that show it is on track, and identifying these at the start will help entrepreneurs track performance and keep important activities in focus. At Weststar, for example, during the busy summer holiday months these indicators were customer retention rate and spend per head in the bars and restaurants. In the winter and spring booking seasons I had to concentrate on the booking figures and capital expenditure to make sure that all the projects to get the parks up and running were on schedule. If the business was to run efficiently, I had to spend 80 per cent of my time on driving those key indicators. The remaining 20 per cent had to be divided among all the other day-to-day projects that make up the running of a business.

It was all too easy to be distracted. I would frequently challenge myself and think: 'What am I doing? How long have I been standing here talking about something irrelevant?' Similarly, when I was sitting in meetings with the team, I used to calculate their combined salaries and tot up in my mind how much money that hour-long meeting had just cost. If the fruits of that meeting did not make the business at least twice the amount of the combined salaries, the equivalent of a 100 per cent mark-up on our time, I felt we had completely wasted it.

Discussing the same point endlessly and going around in circles can cost a business thousands of pounds. I cannot emphasise enough how essential it is to make all meetings productive. There are many types of meeting, but the ones most commonly used in business are the fixed format, operational sort – for example, the weekly marketing update – and the more strategic, creative meetings that are crucial to the future of the business.

In the first type – those about the day-to-day functioning of the business – everyone should know their role as you go over what was decided last week, what effect it has had and what needs to be changed as a result. These meetings should be quick, efficient and effective. I would expect, as a matter of course, that people would arrive fully briefed and up to speed. There is nothing worse than sitting in a room of eight people where there are seven of them who have done the preparation and one who only vaguely knows why they are there. I think it is unforgivable to waste half an hour of everyone else's time to bring that one person up to date. I will always challenge anyone who is floundering because they are underprepared, and in the past I've actually asked such people to leave meetings – there was little point in them being there, after all.

I would, of course, expect the same standards from the person at the top. I wouldn't dream of sitting in a meeting and bluffing my way through it. There have been occasions in my career when I have not had the chance to read all the papers beforehand, but I came clean and worked hard to make sure I remained up to speed. But that situation is rare. I am, after all, paying for these people's time. What sort of fool would I have to be to pay my team to sit there while I catch up?

If the boss arrives at a meeting thoroughly briefed and ready with penetrating questions, it sends out a powerful message to all the people there who are supposed to be experts in their field. I would always try to be ahead of the game to get the most out of every meeting.

The second type of meeting is the less regular strategic meeting, where matters that are important to the future of the business are decided. The main drawback is that people can feel the need to say something – anything – in these meetings, just because they have been invited. In their desire to impress, people often end up repeating what they said at the previous meeting.

I once had a board director who would, without fail, wait until the whole subject of the meeting had been debated and put to bed before opening up the debate again. He didn't like to feel that he hadn't made a contribution, but he was not fond of making decisions. I am wary of people who speak only to make sure that they are heard saying something.

Meetings should be disciplined, and everyone should bear in mind why they are there and why the meeting is being held. Far too many people do not make it clear why they are gathering all their senior staff together, and they have a monthly strategy session simply because it has always been so. That is how things drift. I would want to make absolutely sure that I spent the time discussing the things that mattered to that business at that time. The simple test is to ask: 'Why are we having this meeting? When we walk out of here today, what do we all need to know, what are we going to do, and what difference is this meeting going to make?' It makes perfect sense to send an email to everybody in advance to tell them the purpose of the meeting.

Such meetings generally follow a formal structure, opening with minutes from the last meeting, followed by action points, and then everyone gets the opportunity to air their own points that they want to put on the agenda. I would drop all that. To promote creative thought and get the best out of a meeting, I always turn it on its head. Never, ever start off with the minutes from the last meeting. Delay them to the end, and if the meeting runs out of time then at least the important things have been debated at the start. The 'any other business' section, for example, often contains some of the meatiest stuff, so why not start with that?

Time management is a skill that few people get right and everyone can improve upon. I find it does help to set in my mind how long a task is going to take before I get started. It is surprising how many people don't do that, but that simple step helps to prioritise the task in terms of how important it really is and how much time it deserves.

It takes discipline, and I don't always get it right, but everyone should regularly check themselves and ask whether the task they are undertaking is truly a good use of their time. It was Henry Ford who pointed out that time waste is in some ways worse than material waste because there can be no salvage, and I wholly agree with that.

I have one final point to make about time management, which is that I'm sceptical about the benefits of some modern technology. I don't believe that it is always the panacea it is made out to be for freeing up 'time-poor' executives – it can actually waste a lot of time, too. It drives me crazy when company executives spend all their time emailing or blogging, and then tell me they are too busy to do anything else. Sarah Lu, the entrepreneur behind youdoodoll, used to spend hours maintaining her blog. She is a highly creative and quirky individual, which is entirely in keeping with her fabulous and unusual mini-me doll-making kits, and that is what appealed to me in the first place. She is utterly in touch with the target customer who would appreciate these imaginative dolls and who probably does spend hours online and on networking sites. However, in my view this is not enough of a valid business reason for placing blogging ahead of other critical business issues or putting it at the top of her to-do list. There is, in fact, a fairly narrow group of people who read blogs and then buy the products. I have said to Sarah Lu: 'Is this blog measurable? Are we actually selling any more youdoodolls on the back of it? This is taking up time, and time means money.'

My advice to anyone is to think twice before spending hours blogging about their innermost thoughts and to get on with the tangible activity of actually selling the product to as broad an audience as possible.

. . . and your cash

'The cheque is in the post' is not just one of the greatest lies used in business, it is also a symptom of a far greater problem. When they have cash-flow problems too many companies convince themselves that it will be all right next month and that they just have to wait for X, Y and Z to happen. They never actually work out what the problem is and tackle it. Then, because they have left it too long, it grows into a much larger problem.

Managing cash flow is not something that will just happen in the day-to-day working of the business. It needs to be a business priority, particularly during the tough part of an economic cycle.

People often forget that managing cash flow isn't about accounting, it's about relationships. Being on good terms with your customers and suppliers is the bedrock of an efficient cash flow. It is vital to devote time and energy to building a personal rapport with contacts, otherwise, when times are hard, it is virtually impossible to pick up the phone to ask debtors when they are going to pay the money they owe and get an honest answer. It is the entrepreneurs who have invested time in getting to know the people they work with who will always, inevitably, find themselves near the top of the payments list. This is human nature.

We had firm rules on payment at Weststar. We relied a lot on goodwill in the surrounding areas, so all local suppliers were paid on their payment terms, absolutely bang on the button. The last thing I needed was for a customer to stop at the local garage on the way to one of our parks and hear that 'that lot' up at Mullion never pay their bills on time. In fact, I even made sure that we paid local businesses a little ahead of their terms, so they were always enthusiastic ambassadors for the business. Every business should have a list of suppliers they always pay on time.

Honesty and human contact are the keys when it comes to creditors. If money is temporarily tight, the first task is to work out when the company will be able to pay suppliers. Then pick up the telephone and tell them. If you wait for an impatient supplier to call you, you will already be on the back foot. Being in control goes right to the heart of what it is to be an entrepreneur. Waiting for a situation to get out of hand to the extent that disgruntled suppliers besiege the company goes against everything that entrepreneurs stand for.

Cash will not just flow – it needs to be managed

Of course, during a recession, concerns about cash flow are magnified many times over. While there are no easy fixes in difficult times, there are a number of steps a business can take to protect itself. The first and most obvious of these is not to be afraid to take tough decisions, such as introducing staged delivery of goods – that is, taking smaller deliveries – or making smaller deliveries more often.

Many companies insist on a minimum order because it can be a pain to deliver small or part orders. But, offset that against a climate in which people are less likely to pay on time – or even pay at all in some cases – and it is easy to see that it might be better to inconvenience the business a bit and break some orders down.

As Weststar, for example, we always knew how many guests were coming in the following week, so there was no excuse for the bars and restaurants to be overstocked. All we needed was enough stock to get us through the next three days. Yet sometimes I would walk into the bar cellars and find a season's worth of drink stored there. This might, of course, have been because there had been a special offer, and if we were going to sell it that was absolutely fine, but if we had not known we were definitely going to sell it then it would not have been a good investment.

Youdoodoll has certainly benefited from making staged deliveries. Reducing its minimum order quantity of dolls has worked really well, particularly when we have added something extra for special promotions. So, for example, for Valentine's Day we marketed the reduced minimum order together with a valentine sticker. Shopkeepers loved it because it was a cheap, low-risk way of getting new lines into their shops. They only had to buy ten youdoodolls and it looked as if they had a specific Valentine's Day product. If youdoodoll had a minimum order of 100, stores might not want to take the risk just for Valentine's Day.

Being successful in a recession is all about adjusting trading patterns to reduce the risk for everyone involved. It might mean a bit more work, but it might also be the difference between survival and failure because of falling orders.

It could well be better for a business to make lots of little deliveries, which means that they have less cash at risk, rather than a single big block delivery, which means that everything must be manufactured and paid for up front. It will cost more, because there is additional transport involved and it is not ideal for the environment, but if a company can arrange a delivery every week it won't need to keep two months' stock. And if the product is selling from the outlet that is getting a weekly delivery it is perfectly reasonable to ask the customer for payment before the next delivery is made. Looking carefully at the supply chain is an ideal way of reducing the risk of too much outstanding cash owed by or to third parties.

I would also advise businesses to take a close look at their supply chains and stock levels because in a downturn companies need to be right on the pulse of their stock turnover. All entrepreneurs should know how many days' stock they hold. Cash is tied up in that stock, and if you don't know how much you hold you should put this book down immediately and go and find out. During a recession there are no circumstances in which anyone should be holding six months' stock without a compelling business reason.

If a company suddenly introduced staged deliveries of goods in buoyant times customers would most likely assume that the business was in trouble, but everybody understands that we are in a recession, and businesses around the world are receptive to conversations that would never have happened in more prosperous years. In difficult times it will just be thought of as good management, and everyone knows the risks to their own businesses if the companies they work with fail. In tough economic times there is no way a company should blindly keep on doing more of the same.

Another idea to combat the difficult part of the economic cycle is to consider early settlement discounts. Factor in a slight premium to the price and then offer a 5 per cent discount if a customer settles in 28 days.

I am often asked how I would deal with consistent late payers, and what I say is it doesn't hurt to look at the issue from the other end of the telescope and let the way your company deals with early payers be known more widely. For instance, if there is a limited range or a new product good payers will always get first shot at it. Give customers a genuine incentive to make sure they automatically pay on the button. Even routinely late payers will have a list of people they pay on time, and what a company needs to do is to give a good reason to make sure they are on that list.

It is also perfectly acceptable early on in a start-up business and until a business relationship is fully developed to say that the payment terms are at least 30 per cent up front and 70 per cent on delivery. Larger companies will understand. Alternatively, a business could offer customers a discount if they transfer to regular direct debit payments. What all this means is that the company will be more in control of its cash flow, the bank will feel happier, and the business will be more secure.

There is no way of completely avoiding bad debts, and at some time, particularly during a recession, everyone is going to be caught out, but it is possible to mitigate the circumstances. If a company knows its industry well it is easy to pick up on who does and who doesn't pay on time. Talking to other operators in the market will show a clear consensus on the people in the sector who aren't good with payments.

A potential risk of difficult economic circumstances is that companies become so desperate to open new accounts that they bypass the usual credit-checking systems. No order is 'fantastic' until the customer has paid. If an order is going to put a company at catastrophic risk of debt in order to service it, it is acceptable – indeed, it is understandable – to request a bank guarantee (or a letter of credit if you're exporting) and to check the last set of accounts. Never take on a big order that could turn out to be to the detriment to the rest of the business.

One word of absolute caution is also required here. If the people running the company discover cash-flow problems, they need to identify immediately whether the problems are temporary or terminal. If they are terminal, it's time to start making plans to wind up the business. If, on the other hand, they are temporary, they can be overcome in many different ways. Often, a clear explanation of the situation coupled with a detailed timeline and a plan for recovery will be enough to secure temporary support from a bank or an investor. It is worth remembering, however, that the plan needs to be realistic. Failing to meet it, and having to go back a second or even a third time for additional cash could well spell doom for both the relationship and the business.

It does, of course, help if an entrepreneur is totally familiar with the accounts and the basic day-to-day movements of cash in the company. Oddly, the bookkeeping side of things is often the first thing to slip in start-up businesses. Many entrepreneurs misunderstand accounts and the financial aspect of their business. They find it more fashionable and 'gritty' to fly by the seat of their pants and say that running a company is all about drive, guts and enthusiasm, not numbers. To me, part of being entrepreneurial means having top-notch systems and processes and a strong engine room. If the systems in the engine room are in place an entrepreneur can go off and do edgy, risky things in the knowledge that the business is fundamentally running properly and there are solid indicators to alert them the moment it isn't.

In choosing not to embrace systems and processes, entrepreneurs often comfort themselves by saying that they are too busy going for sales and haven't time for figure work. Whenever I hear those familiar words emanating from one of my investments I know that once I force them into doing a set of management accounts I am likely to find that the business is making great sales but little, if any, profit. It can be a devastating revelation for the entrepreneur.

In the first year of my investment with JPM Eco Logistics the entrepreneurs behind the company kept telling me how well the business was doing yet failed to produce any accounts. When they finally produced a set of detailed year-end figures they were devastated to see that they had lost £77,000. It was then that I discovered what they had meant by 'doing really well'. They were actually saying that turnover was soaring, but the detailed figures quickly made it clear what had been going wrong. The sales margin was far too small because the pricing was wrong. The business was able to re-price in an attempt to get back on track, but it would clearly have been helpful to have done this exercise far earlier.

Oddly, at the time and despite what has happened subsequently, I was quite glad that things came to a head then, because they finally understood why they needed the accountant I had told them to get 12 months earlier. They would be the first to admit that it was a classic early mistake. Until then, they had been trying to muddle through because they did not want to spend money on a bookkeeper.

Another of my investments, reestore, also started off with a somewhat chaotic approach to its numbers. The company designs contemporary, environmentally friendly furniture by taking everyday objects and turning them into something more stylish and original, and I well remember a conversation with Max McMurdo shortly after I invested. Max is a real character and highly creative. He asked me what I thought he should sell a bath-based product for. 'Well,' I asked, 'what do they cost?' He said £20, and it was then that I realised that he meant it cost £20 to buy the raw product, but that was as far as his price breakdown had got. It is hardly surprising that one of the first things that I did with my new investment was to visit his workshop in Bedford to come up with a cost price for his entire catalogue, and this time the sales price reflected not only the cost of the raw materials but also the cost of his time for making each product.

The truth of the matter is that somebody has to watch those numbers. Nobody likes to do bookwork – well, maybe accountants do – but entrepreneurs absolutely have to have a handle on the figures, particularly in the early days. How else can they know when to make the essential tweaks to margins, wages or pricing if there is no indication whatsoever of whether or not the business is profitable? Businesses fail if the people running them have no idea whether they are trading profitably. A company should have somebody sorting out the paperwork, even if it is on a minimal, part-time basis. The person at the helm should see monthly management accounts that are laid out in such a way that they do not require hours of scrutiny. If I am given a set of management accounts I am usually able to identify all the important financial issues in a business within minutes, and I know for a fact that all the other Dragons would say the same thing.

A little bit of knowledge about your business can go a long way, as long as it is the right knowledge. I mentioned earlier in this chapter the key indicators at Weststar. For example, it was set in stone that catering wages should never be more than 20 per cent of gross turnover, whereas those at the bars should never be more than 10 per cent of turnover. It did not matter how well the business appeared to be doing or whether it felt as if it was going through affluent times, I would watch those percentages like a hawk. If I only had a 30-second glance at the management accounts every Friday, the first thing I would look at would be those key performance indicators, and I would instantly know how well the business was trading and whether we needed to take action to get ourselves back on track.

It is the entrepreneurs who take a robust approach to their

finances who show they are in control of their business. Now, more than ever, is the time to get on top of the numbers. Numbers are a symptom of a business. They indicate if it is well and healthy or pretty sick. In a recession companies often don't want to look at the figures because they are afraid of what they may see, but the best advice I can give is to keep an eye on them at all times.

Expect the unexpected

As you can see, there will be plenty enough going on in the day-to-day running of a business to keep any entrepreneur exceedingly busy. Once the company is up and running, it's easy to overlook long-term initiatives in the rush to take care of the short-term issues. However, I would advise anyone to take the time to put together a disaster plan.

Every business will have to find its way through a disaster at some time or other. It could be suddenly finding out that the fruit on sale has been chemically sprayed and could poison someone. It might be a child getting severely injured in a private leisure centre. It could be any one of a thousand possibilities. The point is that every company should consider in depth what would happen in catastrophic circumstances and how it would react.

Disaster planning is not easy, but imagine making decisions and coping with the unexpected on the day that the worst happens, when everyone is panicking and staff are running around like headless chickens. It is far better for the business to consider all the issues in a cool, calm and collected manner beforehand. The trouble is, however, that many companies spend a lot of time talking about needing a recovery plan, but somehow never seem to find the time to prepare one.

The first step is to decide what would constitute a disaster for the business. Not all misfortunes will be catastrophic – someone falling over a box full of stock and breaking an arm should be covered by your insurance, for example. But there are other perils that may seriously affect the company's fortunes – being involved in a serious incident such as a fire, chemical spillage or accidental death, for instance. Every company should sit down and try to identify their most likely catastrophic risks and their response to such an eventuality. It will not be possible to cover every risk, but the recovery plan, which will be produced as a result of this process, should be easily adapted to a range of circumstances.

At Weststar we had a document that was a step-by-step guide for anyone who was in a disastrous or catastrophic situation. It laid out the details and phone numbers of all the senior staff who had to be contacted immediately. It established an information flow and structure and instructed staff that under no circumstances were they to talk to the press and that they should instead direct all media enquiries to the general manager. The manager, in turn, was instructed on how to pass the contact through. The guide set out how and where we would deal with relatives and other people caught up in the incident. It was not a particularly complex or long document, and, as it happened, it spent most of its life on a shelf. But every year we went through it, made any revisions and updates that we thought necessary and made sure it was still relevant. Everyone in the company was aware of the plan; indeed, they knew it so well that if anything had happened nobody would have had to get the document down from the shelf.

One of the situations we planned for and one that did happen twice at Weststar was a massive electricity failure at night. This can, of course, be dangerous if you are staying in a strange caravan. A blackout in a place you don't know can be disorientating, and it is not like being at home where you can pretty much stumble around in the dark to find a torch because you know where everything is.

However, it was not a problem in the park because we had a well-honed plan. We had asked ourselves what could happen and, if it did happen, what everybody would do. We sited emergency generators at the clubroom for just such an eventuality, and when the power cut happened our strategy kicked in. Everyone in the team was dispatched, with torches, to lead the guests to the safety of the clubroom. The guests were given the choice of staying in their caravans with the candles provided until the power was back, but we made it clear that if they wanted to move about the park they had to be escorted for their own safety. The plan worked like a dream. As I said, a complete power failure occurred only twice, but I am sure the guests thought it happened much more often because every member of staff went into automatic mode and was courteous, efficient and in control.

Never forget your goals

I'm always saying that being an entrepreneur is incredibly hard work, and I hope I've given an idea of what that work might entail. Things can get overwhelming, of course, and at that point it is always useful to remember why you went into business in the first place.

During my teenage years my parents bought a lovely derelict millhouse in Wiltshire. It was one of the first obvious signs of the success of their various ventures, and they set about converting it into a home. As they proudly showed me around the large house, which had a glass inset in the floor so you could see the bubbling stream below, I thought: 'So this is what happens if you work hard.'

Money is not, of course, the only motivation for entrepreneurs, which is probably just as well because purely profit-based enthusiasm can wear pretty thin when it becomes a slog. As I have said before, entrepreneurs have to enjoy what they are doing. Top of the list in motivational terms for most small- business founders is the opportunity to run their own show, and this is followed by flexible working hours. It also seems to me to be a wonderful opportunity to create a working environment that chimes with your interests. Unfortunately, as a company becomes more successful it usually gets buried in more red tape, and entrepreneurs may find they have less time to relish the moment or even finish everything that needs to be done.

To keep on an even keel company founders will need to learn to prioritise. If there are three things to be done, they should decide which is the most important and then see if there is someone else who is able to do the other two. Instead of taking an entire task on board, leaders should let someone else do the groundwork and then pick it up again down the line to do the bit they do best.

The greatest danger for entrepreneurs is that they want to get on and do everything. They want it done now and always think they will be better off if they do it themselves. I have often had to check myself as I stand at the photocopier, having thought, 'Oh, it's just a 20-page document. I might as well do it myself.' I have to stop and ask myself, 'Why me?' I have an entire administrative team who are able to do the copying, and standing next to the photocopier is probably not the best use of my time. The trouble is, we entrepreneurs are an impatient bunch.

I think it is the little things, like unnecessary photocopying, that sap the energy of entrepreneurs. If they are not careful, highly motivated company managers can put themselves in a position where they work so hard they make themselves ill. Whatever happened to that dream of flexible working?

Regular short breaks, delegation and prioritisation are the keys to staying motivated and keeping ideas fresh. Stress can undermine motivation. I would urge all entrepreneurs to try to control stress levels by setting realistic goals. They should also give themselves a break now and then, dig out the business plan and pat themselves on the back for their achievements. Staying motivated can be as important as funding or business skills because without it it may be too tough to stay the course.

Setting goals should also mean having a realistic look at how the business will grow. One of the biggest hurdles a business has to overcome is the transfer from one-man band to a large, functioning operation. Funnily enough, after jumping through hoops to raise finance, finding a way to manufacture and then market their product and finally launching it on the world, what often stumps people is taking their business to the next stage.

All this may seem a distant dream to an entrepreneur who is just starting out, but how a business expands to the next stage of growth is something that should be planned well ahead of time. It is hardly surprising that after all the work that goes into getting a business off the ground many entrepreneurs tend to end up emotionally attached to it. It seems impossible to them that one day they might lose control. Those who do reluctantly decide to give up some aspect of the day-to-day running as a company expands usually opt to hand over the parts they don't like, such as sales or talking to customers on the phone, rather than give up the things that they should really not be doing, such as emptying the bins and doing the photocopying. This can be fatal for a fledgling operation. If there is one thing that makes a business tick it is the relationships that the principals have with customers and suppliers. This is a time that the business is forming the culture that will see it through the years to come. If the founder loses control of the relationships and the way the business interacts with the outside, it will push the company off track before it has even found a firm footing.

I would urge all entrepreneurs to plan for growth and the ways in which their role may change. They should also never lose sight of the strengths that they bring to their venture, but equally they need to be aware of the moment that their inability to let go starts to hold the business back.

Create a culture you can be proud of

One of the brilliant things about starting up a new business is that you have the ability to influence the culture of the company from the word go. In recent years environmentally friendly practices and ethical trading have become not only big news but also, seemingly, big business. We've seen many large companies trumpeting their turnarounds in making their practices more acceptable to today's customers, but when you're starting from scratch you can build in these ideas from day one.

I meet a lot of entrepreneurs who are keen to work these issues into their business plans. *Dragons' Den* attracts all sorts of would-be entrepreneurs from many different walks of life and with a huge range of ideas, from the frankly absurd to some truly innovative products, but one thing is always certain and that is that if a product has even the slightest connection with the environment or ethical trading practices, I will be the focus of that entrepreneur's pitch.

It happens every time. Having done their homework, the pitcher will carefully go down the line of Dragons, highlighting what might be of interest to each one of us. So, for example, they might try to persuade Duncan Bannatyne of potential leisure applications, while Theo Paphitis will be told about a product's retail potential in glowing terms, and James Caan is the target for all things in personnel. When it comes to my turn, the entrepreneur will look me in the eyes and say: 'And Deborah, not only is it a brilliant product, it is also environ-mentally friendly.'

It is widely known that I am concerned about waste and the effect it has on the environment. It is a subject that I feel passionate about, and I am keen to encourage everyone to do whatever they practically can. However, while I would never put my money into a product that is significantly harmful to the environment, it is certainly not the most important basis on which I weigh up my investments.

Occasionally, however, I do see a product that ticks all the right boxes and has the bonus of being eco-friendly, and I find that really exciting. When Paul Tinton of Prowaste Management Services presented to the Den in series six I could immediately see that there would be a great demand for the idea behind his business of stopping construction waste being sent to landfill sites by teaching industrial building sites how to sort their recyclable waste correctly. Paul's company then collects the waste products, takes them off to the relevant recycling places and provides the necessary certification, leaving the construction teams to do what they do best, which is construct.

On the face of it, a waste-collecting business is not the most glamorous or interesting sector to get involved with, but, as well as having a great business plan, Paul was extremely impressive, and I immediately felt I could trust him. He also did not strike me as a man who would compromise on the detail. Paul really knew his stuff and had clearly seriously engaged with the environmental issues. I really tested him (he later said he was surprised at the level of testing that came his way), and he passed with flying colours.

Duncan and I each offered him £100,000 for 20 per cent each of the business because we could see that Prowaste was in the right place at the right time. It is a great business, which is absolutely of the moment.

I think it's great that the environment is now 'fashionable', because I do believe that it deserves more attention, but the downside is that some companies see it as an opportunity to jump on the bandwagon when they actually have little interest in or

Resist greenwashing

knowledge of the real issues. Businesses are getting too carried away by the wave of media interest in the environment. They see that most people are scared stiff about the effects of climate change, and they rush to prove their environmental commitment. Companies large and small are falling over themselves to advertise their green credentials.

Well, if they don't realise it already, I have news for these companies. The strategy is not working because the consumer is no fool. People buy products, first and foremost, because they like them. They won't use their hard-earned cash to buy sackcloth and ashes simply because they are environmentally friendly. For example, I try hard to dress in ethically produced, environmentally friendly clothing, but even though I am in the fortunate position of having a stylist who goes out to hunt such pieces down, I have found that most of them are hideous and badly designed. Being eco-friendly should not be an excuse for poor product development or design, but sadly it all too often is.

The very consumers whom firms are relentlessly targeting with their green claims are becoming fed up. In 2008 the Advertising Standards Agency reported that the number of complaints relating to green and environmental statements had quadrupled since the year before. The claims that infuriated consumers most were that products or services were carbon 'neutral', 'zero' or 'negative'. Pronouncements that goods were 100 per cent recyclable or wholly sustainable were also frequently challenged.

As the recession begins to bite, I predict that these 'greenwash' claims will slow down. Companies and consumers have other things on their minds. However, I would always advocate getting the company's eco-house in order so that customers will not only have the option of buying something that they like and want but also get the feel-good factor that they are buying something that is not causing long-term harm to the planet.

To be truly green a company must be committed to improving things. One way to do this is to sign up to the Carbon Trust Standard, a Kitemark for green businesses, which I helped to launch in June 2008. To be certified a company has to commit to reducing its emissions every year, filling out a four-stage application form and agreeing to be independently assessed. This accreditation, like the Fairtrade and organic stamps, has a real resonance with consumers. It takes a company away from the rather unsubstantiated claims that flood the world of greenwash and into the realms of being a serious eco-player.

Some start-up companies have claimed that they can't afford to be ethical or environmentally friendly, but building these principles into the company from the outset can often save money. Creating a carbon footprint, burning fossil fuels and paying landfill taxes cost money and hit profits, so it is far better to avoid them if you can.

A good tip for start-ups keen to tackle ethical trading by way of their supply base is to piggyback their operation on to a path forged by other, more established manufacturers. They should look at the factories and suppliers that major corporations are dealing with, where they are and how they operate. It would be safe to rely on the fact that commercial giants, such as Waitrose and IKEA, which trade on their ethical credentials, have done their homework when it comes to finding factories and will probably have done more research than a small operation could ever possibly hope to do.

Once start-ups get a picture of which the approved suppliers are, they should approach them and ask for details of their background, their certification and verification of the companies for which they currently manufacture goods. I confess to a certain amount of self-interest here. Because I have taken such a publicly ethical stance, it would not do to be seen to be investing in a business that was not without reproach. When I first invested in youdoodoll the dolls were being made by Sarah Lu's aunt in the UK. Clearly this could not continue because we were confident that there would be a huge surge in demand, yet the cost of scaling up production in Britain was going to be high and meant that the price we would need to charge would be prohibitive. We therefore had to balance the environmental advantages of production at home against the business issues of price. Having considered all the pros and cons, we made a decision to source the products in China. After extensive research we chose a factory with excellent ethical and environmental credentials that also makes Disney toys. The difference in price between that and another factory without such good references was a matter of pennies. So, not only did it make little difference to the bottom line, but it also fitted the personal values of both the company's founder and me.

If a company is set up as an ethical business it is well worth applying for a stamp of approval from an organisation like the

Being ethical is not an indulgence

Ethical Trading Initiative (ETI). The ETI is an alliance of companies, non-governmental organisations (NGOs) and trade union organisations that aims to promote and improve supply-chain working conditions and international labour standards. The most important thing about an ethical business is the way the business behaves and the way it is seen to behave by consumers. Often obtaining these marks takes time, so it is useful to start behaving that way and the stamp will follow later.

Sometimes following your principles when it comes to environmentally friendly and ethical trading means adding a bit more to the cost of your product. If this is the case it's really important to communicate to your customers why the product is selling at a premium. If this is the message at the heart of a company it should make sure that it is aired loud and clear, so that when people are making their purchasing decisions they have all the information in front of them to help them decide. However, be absolutely sure of the grounds on which you make the claim. Taking claims at face value is a dangerous route to go down, and something that is supposed to help build a business can quickly destroy it.

Personally, I believe that all businesses, no matter which sector they are in, should look at their company from an ethical viewpoint. If everyone were to work with responsible suppliers who pride themselves on being ethical and environmentally friendly the short-sighted ones who do not care about these issues will eventually fail. Being ethical is not an indulgence, and when it becomes part of a company's character it is not hard work at all. Once a firm starts thinking ethically it becomes part of its thought processes, its character and its culture.

'Be proactive, not reactive'

A good company runs on a mixture of proactive and reactive initiatives. It should keep ahead of the game by judging the market and forecasting what will be important to its customers in the future, and it should also take the temperature of what is making them tick right now. In truth, no matter how well entrepreneurs think they know a given market, the consumer will always surprise them. There will be a sudden shift in public opinion or something out of the ordinary will capture the customers' imaginations, and it is up to the market to react swiftly to the change. As long as a business responds quickly and effectively, everything is fine. There is no problem whatsoever with being reactive. It is standing still and ignoring the zeitgeist that is the real crime in business.

Chapter 7
Building your team

I have few fond memories of my time at boarding school in Wincanton. The most positive part of this episode in my life was an amazing teacher, whom we knew as Miss Jefferies. She was not kind or soft, but her sense of fair play was truly remarkable and an inspiration to all those around her. She was also highly creative in the way she taught and was able to engage children of all abilities, finding a way to encourage all of us, whatever our skill level. But, woe betide the pupil who did not work hard, try hard and commit fully. She left a deep impression on me and, I am sure, contributed towards the sense of fairness that has dominated my career.

As a consequence of her firm but fair approach, I worked hard in Miss Jefferies' lessons. Indeed, I worked hard in any lesson where the teacher impressed me, and, I confess, rather took my foot off the gas in the classes where I thought the teacher was too soft or not really up to the job. Of course, with a change of teacher in different subjects each year it meant that some years I excelled in one subject and the next I would be at the bottom of the class. My father, Brian, said that reading my end-of-term school reports was like looking into the life of a schizophrenic.

On reflection, I know I have taken this attitude into my business career. If someone impresses me I will go to extraordinary lengths to work with them and help them succeed, but if I can see that they haven't got what it takes I am open and honest with them. What really bothers me, however, is when I come across people who have got what it takes but who refuse to apply themselves. I rarely give these people much of my time. The only difference now is that I often do a personal 'sense check' to make sure that I am not being too quick to judge and write off someone who might otherwise impress.

Finding the right people to work with can be difficult, particularly, it seems, for entrepreneurs, who tend to be rather keen on being in control. When people start businesses they tend not to get people in soon enough. While the business is in the growing phase and everyone is watching the pounds and the pennies they do not prepare for the next phase. If there is a clear picture of where the business is going, there has to be a plan of how to get there. Hire ahead of expansion, because if one thing is certain it is that companies without enough people will not reach their goals.

Entrepreneurs who are on the cusp of beginning to recruit generally feel a combination of relief that they are no longer going it alone and fear that they are going to have to let go of some of their precious venture. They will, of course, have to overcome this fear in order to take the business forward, and I actually think this is one of the moments in a business's life when it is easy to spot

Nobody works best alone

whether someone is a genuine entrepreneur. True entrepreneurs will realise that they are stopping the business from growing and that they need people around them.

I am good at most things, but I am not the best at any. I recognise and am prepared to admit that there is always somebody who is better than me. To achieve the best results, all I have to do is make sure that I gather round me enough people who have the sort of expertise that I require.

Hiring for skill

It is amazing how many entrepreneurs make the error of hiring for convenience or roping in friends and family simply because it looks like an easier, cheaper option. When one of my investors says to me, 'It's OK, I've got a mate on board to do a favour for me and get this job sorted,' my heart sinks. An entrepreneur who is trying to get a quality service or product into the marketplace has to be able to hold everyone involved to account. Every person who is connected to the project has to commit to getting things done on time and delivered to the specifications, and it is difficult to insist on timings and delivery criteria when someone is doing the company a favour. And it's even harder to fire a friend or family member if they are just no good at the job.

An example of this is a high-profile launch that I held for one of my investments. In addition to a good number of journalists from the national press, we were expecting a significant turnout of celebrities. Nothing was left to chance, and professionals were hired for virtually every aspect of the event to make sure that it went smoothly. The entrepreneur involved was keen to keep costs down and offered to bring some friends in to man the bar. Stupidly, I agreed. Three days before launch day I could already see that we had a problem. We had no feedback from these friends whatsoever and didn't even know if they were going to turn up. Normally, if I am paying someone, this is the stage where I would pick up the phone and demand an immediate face-to-face meeting. But when it is a friend and they are not being paid to do a job what can you do? Sure enough, the friends did not show up, and everyone was left with an extra layer of stress sorting out last-minute replacements.

I would always think carefully about accepting favours. It might seem an attractive option in the difficult, early days, but remember: if this business is worth giving up everything for, presumably it is worth paying some money to give it the best possible start.

When I am recruiting I always look for people who have something more than just their individual narrow skills. I like people who are not simply administrators or marketers or sales-people but who can take a much wider view as well. This is essential in a start-up when often there are times when you need all hands to the pump. If a company is not careful and recruits people who each have their own individual specialisations, things can quite quickly break down into little fiefdoms. The company ends up with the strongest personalities ruling the roost and having far too much influence over the business. In fact, the personalities need to step out of it, and everyone has to do what is right for the business. Forget who shouts loudest.

Communication, communication, communication

The person at the top has to understand the ebb and flow of a business and find a way to communicate and inspire the team at all levels, but when you've put together a talented team it makes sense to listen to what they have to say. In those early days at Weststar, flushed with ideas of what I could do with the business, I produced a ten-point, company-wide mission statement. I pinned it to the wall with a flourish and quickly set out to convey the message. Within days, if not hours, I realised it was completely irrelevant. In fact, while we all had one vision, different parts of the business needed different missions.

At that time there was a head office, five holiday parks and a wide range of people doing all sorts of different jobs. We were providing a great holiday experience, but our individual roles in providing that experience were entirely different. There was absolutely no point conveying the message to the maintenance department that our objective was to answer the phone within three rings – they rarely received telephone calls. However, if we had told them that we wanted to be seen to be quick and courteous at all times, that would have been entirely relevant to them. The goal of the company is that we all do the same thing, but we all need to know how our individual contribution is relevant. The trick is to convey that message down the line so that everyone buys into it and doesn't think it is simply a faceless diktat from the fun factory that is head office. (I do not, in fact, like the term 'head office' because the real function of the business takes place at the customer end. If it has to have a title at all I would call it 'central office', which is what we did at Weststar.)

Remember to listen

What is most important is that everybody is proud of what their company does and what their company is going to do. They do not need a notice pinned to the wall. The mission, or indeed vision, should be conveyed in the way a company speaks, walks, thinks and dresses. It is the entire ethos of the company. Everyone should be living it, breathing it and acting it. What is pinned up on the wall is by the by because it is so completely obvious that they know what they are doing.

It is important to understand that different parts of the business are on a different rhythm and flow and need to be addressed in a different way if they are going to buy into the vision. That requires time, skill, experience and, every so often, leaving your ego at home.

If you are listening to your employees' ideas you should also be alert to how they feel about their role within the business. People know when they are being underpaid and quickly learn to resent it. I have always worked with people who work so far above and beyond the call of duty that it is simply not right not to pay them enough. That is simply taking advantage of them. If a company wants to build up a good team it should consider paying above the going rate. I don't mean paying ridiculously high salaries, however; that can be just as counterproductive because employees who feel they are overpaid constantly worry that they will be found out and their job will be at risk. I would research the sector and compare the remuneration for the post on offer with other jobs in the area. I would then make it known to the employee that they are at the top of, maybe even slightly above, the going rate. I am open with my employees so that they understand where they sit on the pay scale.

It is often, however, not simply about pay. I have known people who are paid well yet are extremely dissatisfied in their jobs. Some have even left to take a job with a lower salary. I feel that what they are looking for is that combination of feeling that their job is worthwhile and that they are appreciated, which is reflected in the right salary. Employees need to feel good about what they are doing and at the same time know that what they produce each day has credibility. There are a number of ways of achieving this, and the first, most obvious way – also free – is feedback. If they have done a good job, tell them how good they are and how pleased the company is with what they have done. A little praise goes a long way, and it raises the morale of the whole team. Similarly, if they have underperformed, tell them that. Otherwise, if all a company leader does is hand out praise the words quickly become almost meaningless.

Rather than being known as 'nice', I'd much rather be seen as fair, which is a lesson that dominated my childhood. As well as Miss Jefferies at school, who drummed a feeling of fair play into her pupils, there was also the period when Gail and I were sent to live with a wonderful family for six months when my mother was working too many hours to be able to look after us. Auntie Angela and Uncle Derek, as we called them, had four daughters of their own, yet their most endearing quality was a tremendous sense of fairness, and that had a massive, long-lasting impact on me. They treated Gail and me as equal to their own children, and I will never forget that lesson nor how good it felt. I never, ever play favourites.

At Weststar the whole of the senior team was on the Shadow Share Bonus scheme in addition to the company bonus scheme. The scheme was structured to help them concentrate on their own individual areas but at the same time to take a much wider view of the interests of the company. Every year the company put a percentage of profits into the pot that was to be distributed among the senior team. The team's individual targets were based on the amount they contributed to that pot, and the percentage never changed, so if they all did really well, that could affect the size of the pot and it would get bigger in money terms. While they concentrated on the day-to-day running of their own departments, they were also forced to look at the greater good of the company. If, for example, Department X wanted £100,000 for one project and Department Y wanted £100,00 for a different project but the total budget available was only £100,000, they had the incentive to decide among themselves which strategy had the stronger case. They were compelled to examine the wider picture and decide which route would have the better effect.

Another aspect of the Shadow Share Bonus scheme was that if the company was sold, at exit a percentage of the pot would be distributed among the senior management team. This forced them to think about the long-term good of the business, knowing that, one day, they would like the business to be worth X amount of money. They were tied in to the future fortunes of the business because, all being well, that would be where the big money lay.

The checks and balances of the scheme made sure the team was never completely focused on one area or simply dreaming about the day the company was sold, and it worked well to make sure the whole team kept working together.

It's also essential to develop a staff performance appraisal system that works. I'm not a big fan of the formal approach of filling out lengthy forms and spending hours going over and over the same thing. Apart from anything else, I think this encourages managers to see the appraisal process as a time-consuming task that interrupts more 'important' activities. Employees sense this and then feel undervalued and demotivated before the process even begins.

When I'm doing appraisals I always put the onus on people to assess their own performance. If I need to discuss anything negative, I try to be clear and concise and ask questions rather than make statements. People are often surprisingly honest when they have to talk about themselves to somebody else. I try to get them to say how they think their work has gone, what they have achieved so far and what they hope to achieve in the future, and also to describe why something might have gone wrong or why it worked so well. It is much better and more powerful if an employee concludes for themselves that they have not got something right rather than hearing it from the person at the top. It gives the business owner the opportunity to respond and encourage their team to get things right next time.

I would add a word of caution here that I wish everyone would heed. In an attempt to keep their appraisals positive I have often come across managers who employ the method of tempering bad news with good. Most people have come across this method in the past, and it takes the form of the appraiser starting with, 'You have done a really good job, but . . .'. This is bad practice. Bad news is bad news, and good is good. Using this muddled approach can cause the employee to disregard the good news, and in any case it sends a confusing message. It is far better to pay them the respect of being honest, direct and fair. After all, when they leave the room you want them to act on the discussions you have just had, not wonder what it was you have just said and what it all meant.

I would always shy away from directly linking the appraisal process with the annual pay review. The two are obviously related, because if an employee is not doing well it will affect their pay prospects, but if there is too much emphasis on the financial side everyone immediately becomes defensive of their position. Start the appraisal process six months before the pay review and tell the employee that if they want to maximise their opportunity for a pay rise, this is what they have to do. Give them a chance to do something about their performance and be open about it.

Create a happy working environment

Most of us spend at least half our daily lives in the workplace, which means that employers have a considerable responsibility to create an environment in which people can enjoy themselves and feel good about their work. I have learned to speak in terms of 'we' when I'm discussing the activities of the various businesses I am involved with. It can be immensely powerful. I try to create a reasonably informal environment, with some structure, just as people would get in their own homes. I avoid laying down rules but instead make it clear that the business has a culture that dictates what is acceptable.

Work should be fun. It is hard at times, so why not have a sense of humour about it? Of course, it is not all a giggle and a joke. I do have high expectations of people, but employees like having a lot expected of them. Too many people spend their lives being told that they are underachievers, and pretty soon they develop low self-esteem. When they work for somebody who genuinely expects them to do well it is actually quite flattering, and they generally rise to the occasion.

We were all born with the belief that we can do anything, but from that first day we are constantly taught what we cannot do.

A teacher from a school in London's East End recently contacted me about just that. She said she was a great admirer of *Dragons' Den* and uses my work and achievements as an example for her young female students who often don't believe they can have a career outside of getting married and having children and drop out. She told me that the main problem they have is that they are constantly being reminded that they have limits. Her argument is that they should stop making their own limits because they will get enough of them in the real world.

This teacher is an inspiration, and the philosophy she is advocating should be replicated in every workplace. Staff should not be allowed to start filtering out their own abilities because they think it is impossible to achieve anything and there are too many barriers to overcome. When they say, 'I don't think I will be able to do X or Y,' a good employer will reply, 'Have a go, because I think you can.' Then they will create an environment that will help them every step of the way.

Making people feel good about their work is the best way to motivate them. Although pay is an important factor in bringing the team together and pushing them towards a common goal, what is more important is to make people feel that they are part of something exciting.

I don't take any prisoners, though. If I have recruited badly and find out that my new employee is just sloppy and doesn't care, I don't tolerate it. It is not just for my sake; it is also because all the other people in the company would feel cheated. They would think, 'Wait a minute. Deborah expects a lot of me, but how come this new person is allowed to get away with that kind of behaviour?' It is the job of the person at the top not to allow one person to let down the rest of the team.

A final note of caution is needed here. While I would do anything in my power to make sure that all members of my team are happy and fulfilled, I am wary of building a group that is so cliquey and tight-knit that the customer becomes irrelevant. It is fine on a personal and private basis – I am sure a night out with my sisters and me is a nightmare because we do form an impenetrable, cliquey group – but it is totally unacceptable in a business setting. We've all been in businesses like it. The staff look cheerful and well looked after, but, as a customer, you feel embarrassed to be intruding on their club-like space. It is unattractive because it creates the feeling that they are on the inside and the customer is not. In this situation I half imagine that the team gets so self-confident about what a good time they are having and what a marvellous company it is that they might, at any moment, turn to the customer and say, 'Well, what do *you* want?'

It can be difficult to achieve the right balance because, of course, staff should be able to have fun. An example of the way we resolved it at Weststar was to encourage bar staff to join in with the entertainment in the clubrooms. While the bands were playing or when the acts were on stage we positively wanted our people to dance, sing, invent silly routines and interact with the guests. They were given carte blanche to be completely involved with what was going on in the clubroom. But the moment the music stopped they knew that they had to return to their posts and serve drinks. Staff should always be encouraged to enjoy themselves as long as that enjoyment enhances the customers' experience. Visible fun and antics should be encouraged – but only at the appropriate time.

I would contrast this with Marks & Spencer, which I had always cited as one of the UK's most cliquey retailers until the present chief executive, Sir Stuart Rose, took over. Before then, staff definitely appeared to feel as if they were more important than the customers. The chain had spent so much time and energy trying to make its staff feel special that it had completely lost its way, and no one bothered to think of the customer.

If the employees are enjoying themselves in a way that is inclusive, it is brilliant for everyone all round. After all, who can be a better ambassador for a business than an employee who genuinely believes in the product? But if customers feel that they are getting in the way, that happy business has a real problem.

Another aspect that I like to encourage in the working culture of my businesses is the space to make mistakes. If a business is being proactive, putting its head on the line and doing everything in its power to please its customers, some things are going to fail. Both success and failure happen to everyone all day, every day. As long as you win more than you lose, you're on the right track. Indeed, if I were to summarise the key to entrepreneurial success, I would say just that: get more right than you get wrong.

There is a lovely anecdote about Larry Page, the co-founder of Google, who was told by a colleague that she had made a mistake that had cost the company millions of dollars. Instead of blowing his top, he apparently replied: 'I'm so glad you made this mistake because I want to run a company where we are moving too quickly and doing too much, not being too cautious and doing too little. If we don't have any of these mistakes, we're just not taking enough risk.'

When I started in the Den one of my former Weststar team was interviewed as part of a newspaper profile on me. He said that I had created an environment at the holiday parks in which it was all right to try but fail provided the whole thing had been well considered and rationally thought out. I could not have been more gratified to hear a comment like that.

Another key aspect of the environment I aimed to create at Weststar was to allow some flexible working. Staggered hours or term-time working with unpaid leave during the holidays make complete sense for those with young children, but despite a wealth of legislation aimed at opening up better practices, there is still too little provision of flexible arrangements. Forget for a moment any male versus female, battle of the sexes stereotypes. Isn't it just madness not to use a resource like experienced men and women who have worked at a good level elsewhere just because they have got children? Why wouldn't you want to use them?

Flexible hours must work for both parties, of course, but in the current difficult climate adopting flexibility could be a real resolution to the peaks and troughs of demand. Indeed, a good working relationship thrives on a certain amount of back-scratching. In other words, if someone helps out with the business requirements, then when they need help the business will help them out with their personal requirements. But, the balance must be seen to be fair and to work well for both parties. Problems arise when one party feels they are being abused or taken for granted.

My advice is to make the whole process transparent and fair within a business. There will always have to be a core of full-time, permanent staff, but there should be room for a fixed number of part-time, flexible roles. There should be no envy or sniping as long as everybody in the company has the same opportunities at different times in their lives and it is understood that the business has, say, only six part-time positions at any given time. After all, most people who work full-time have to, or want to, while those who work part-time may do so because at that time that is all their circumstances will allow. In my experience, being flexible is actually cost-effective and helps to get the most out of what will inevitably become a more contented and motivated workforce. Being fair and investing trust in an employee's potential can go a long way.

One of the things that can really disrupt a happy working environment is bullying, a pet hate of mine. I've seen bullying in my organisations both within the team and from suppliers who try to put pressure on my employees to buy their product. I have even had experience of people trying to bully me. It can take many different forms, from mild, when people can easily be asked to tone it down a bit, to full-on finger-jabbing or mental bullying. I will not tolerate any type of bullying in any circumstances.

One of my most memorable cases involved a supplier to Weststar. We were updating our booking systems, so we were working closely with an outside company that was designing and installing the new system. The representative from that supplier, with whom we were dealing on a day-to-day basis, turned out to be an extremely opinionated bully. While it didn't bother me immediately, because my project manager was working with him most of the time, insisting on the way we needed things done, it soon became evident that the supplier was completely unwilling to change the way his system worked to suit our needs. His way around this was to try and bully us into changing our systems and processes to make his life easier, even though it would make our life and, more importantly, our customers' lives more difficult.

Like most bullies, he did not even attempt to take on my project manager, who was a strong, positive and intelligent person and who, absolutely rightly, was having none of it. No, our contact decided to tackle the more vulnerable junior members of the booking team. I came into the office one day to find him yelling at one of the youngest members of the booking team to the point of making her cry. His stance was clear. He was trying to make her, and indeed the rest of the team, feel stupid because they couldn't make his system work properly. He wanted to convince them that the only reason for this was because they did not have the capacity to understand it, not that it was an unworkable system.

Adopt a zero tolerance approach to bullying

I immediately confronted him, and, of course, he just crumbled, saying there was a misunderstanding. There was no misunderstanding. This man was a bully, and I demanded that he be removed from the job. The suppliers were told to provide someone who did what we required and made what we wanted happen or they too would be off the project.

Most people think bullying happens only within an organisation. It doesn't. It happens a lot everywhere in business, and it is up to a company manager to keep an eye out for it. The team must know that they are employed in a culture where bullying won't be tolerated. That sort of behaviour can happen only when it is allowed to and when people feel that they haven't got anyone to tell or to turn to. I hope that, following my public displays against bullying, my team will always feel confident enough to know I would always react.

When tough times come you must meet them head-on

There is no doubt that we are currently in the downward side of a long-term economic cycle, and if there is anything wrong with your business you will not be able to count on limping along until things get better. It could, and probably will, be years before the economy picks up again, so making sure that the business is efficient at all levels is important to everyone's jobs, because, to repeat my oft-quoted mantra, it has never been more important to look after the business because the business will look after everyone in it. In other words: review the business, make a plan and act fast if you want to reduce the effect of the downturn.

There are hardly any businesses, and I include some of my own here, where I have not walked in and asked myself: 'Who are all these people? What do they all do? What are they actually responsible for?' While there is often a tendency for entrepreneurs to delay employing people, it can quickly go to the other extreme when trading is good. After not having enough people, a business suddenly goes on a roll and fills every job it can think of and more besides. Business owners justify it in their heads by saying: 'Oh, it might only be a half-job, but this person can also do so and so too.' Before they know it, they have far too many people. Some even become quite egotistical about it and boast that they employ, say, 300 people. 'Yes,' I feel like asking, 'but what are they all doing?'

In more buoyant times many managers indulge themselves by building up large teams in the belief that this somehow reflects their importance or perhaps, in the most basic form, simply makes their lives easier. However, in a harsh economic climate such decisions are as ludicrous as they are wasteful and demotivating for all concerned. In a downturn people are far more likely to be willing to pull together and work that bit harder than employ an extra person and add to the strain on the company at a difficult time.

Some members of the team might welcome working fewer hours, and there may be an opportunity to help employees who have always dreamed of starting up their own business. In my own case, for example, I employed a really excellent girl in my booking office at Weststar who wanted to start up her own training business. One year, when the business was considering cutting back, I offered her a guaranteed two days a week work with me plus a training contract while she went out and fulfilled her dream. She jumped at the chance, and I had a happy part-time booking clerk.

There are often times when a leader has to act in the best interests of the business, even though it might cause some pain to the employees, because if the business doesn't survive, none of the jobs will survive. There might be a case for asking if a group of people would be willing to accept a four-day week. Business leaders should not be frightened of tackling the question because if they have the conversation early on, there may be a chance of finding a workable solution. It may mean that even though nobody is truly happy, nobody is absolutely devastated.

If there is no option but to cut jobs, redundancies should be handled sensitively and carefully, and it's important that the company always operates within the legal framework.

I would recommend getting the news out to the whole company as soon as the decision is taken because the whole workforce will get to know pretty soon anyway, and maintaining a stoic silence from the top team is a sure way of getting destructive rumours started. The process begins by informing employees what is going on, why job cuts are necessary, in which category they will fall and the procedure that will be followed to select them. It is important to be clear about the time period for the process.

The next step is to ask employees if they would consider voluntary redundancy. The advantage of this is that anyone who is unhappy is bound to put up their hand first. Of course, this can backfire, and the company might find a really important member of the team volunteering to go. It is also worth considering whether it will be possible to offer people alternative positions in the business. In that case, the new jobs must be similar in skills, pay, benefits and conditions in order to satisfy legal requirements.

During the subsequent consultation period you will need to tell the employees who are facing compulsory redundancy what the selection criteria are, when it will happen and how much they are likely to receive in redundancy pay. They should be given adequate time to think it over and the opportunity to return and challenge the selection. At the end of the process, however, if you cannot come to an agreement, it is up to the company to issue a dismissal notice.

Redundancy is obviously a traumatic experience for everyone, and it is up to the management to handle it in the most sensitive manner possible. For most entrepreneurs it will be a new and unwelcome experience. I would recommend that anyone in this situation prepares fully and takes advice.

Having to make people redundant is one of the most unpleasant aspects of running a business, and having to fire someone who is simply not up to scratch or is perhaps even a real liability to the business is not much better. It is usually possible to spot a recruitment mistake fairly rapidly. For example, at Weststar we had a clear annual cycle because the business was so seasonal. In one year we saw somebody operate in each mode, so by the time the following year came around I would be expecting the new recruit to be making a visible impact on the business. Other businesses might have an operating cycle of four months or two years. The point is that, no matter what the company's cycle, if the new employee is not learning or bedding in, the person at the top has to think fast and act decisively.

Like everyone, I have made recruiting errors, but I have always quickly resolved them. I will not live with bad decisions.

There is a good deal of legislation to negotiate when it comes to firing people, however, and I would always take advice from a trade body or lawyer. The Federation of Small Businesses, for example, has a very good service that will talk a company through the process and insure against any potential losses. Often, though, it is quickest and cheapest to agree a financial settlement on the understanding that the employee leaves immediately. I would insist on a compromise agreement, which takes the form of a legal document stating that the terms were in full and final settlement.

A lot of companies feel that they have to find a replacement for an unsatisfactory employee before they dismiss them, and this means the whole process can drag on far too long. Once the decision is taken that someone has to go, I would act immediately. Junior employees can easily step up to the plate for a short period, and indeed they often see it as an opportunity to prove themselves. I have found some really good senior staff in this way.

When staff are made redundant or are dismissed it is important not to forget that the people left behind will feel nervous and unsettled. I would be honest with them and tell everyone that the business is overstaffed. If you explain that, for example, the reason there have been no pay rises is because there are six too many people in the company and steps have to be taken to address the problem, staff will see it in a different light. No matter how much people dislike seeing a treasured colleague go, they will accept it if they can see it is affecting their own position.

'Surround yourself with people smarter than you'

Company leaders are not looking for a bunch of really clever people who can outwit them at every turn. They are looking for people who have particular strengths in a specific area. By all means, find people with talent who are smarter than you in their particular areas, but stay one step ahead by being smarter overall.

Chapter 8
Building your brand

At first sight it looked like a terrific sales coup. LateralCorp, a Devon-based fashion distribution business, had secured a deal with one of the UK's trendiest clothing chains. I had been working with the company, which was formed by a group of fashion experts at the turn of the millennium, for just a few months by the summer of 2008, and everyone was excited by the opportunity.

LateralCorp specialises in successful clothing brands such as WeSC, RVCA and Keep, and this seemed to be just the break it had been waiting for. By any account, the youth-orientated retail chain was the perfect market for their products. So, why was it that I and the fashion consultant whom I had brought on board as part of my investment advised them to turn it down?

The chain was planning to stock one of LateralCorp's most successful T-shirt designs and had ordered 500 of them for one store in London. The problem for us was that by selling just one design in a massive shop there was a huge risk that it would be lost in the mass of eye-catching brands. There was a serious possibility that shoppers would never spot the T-shirts and therefore never buy one. In addition, LateralCorp would not be getting brand exposure at this important time of its expansion; it would simply be getting T-shirt exposure. It could destroy the brand before it was even given a chance to fly. It was hard to see why the chain would ever buy any further stock because LateralCorp had no real brand awareness and no credible sales.

In a bold move, LateralCorp returned to the clothing chain to renegotiate. Fuelled by the knowledge that the T-shirt range was clearly in demand, LateralCorp said it would sell the required stock only if the chain also agreed to sell a further 15 items in the range. There is nothing so enticing in the fashion business as someone saying 'no'. It is an industry that thrives on people desiring the things they can't have. The deal wasn't struck immediately, but LateralCorp has now secured substantial orders.

Many companies, not just relatively new ones like LateralCorp, can find themselves faced with a similar conundrum. When a company is keen to sell its goods or sign what looks like a great deal it is all too easy to agree to an order from virtually anybody. The problem is that, when building a brand and a business, it is important to have a plan of who the company will sell to and the way the products will be sold.

I would go so far as making a list of the top ten prospects and the type of businesses they are. If the 'wrong' people apply to buy the product, a company needs to think long and hard about whether they are going to sell to them, because one badly thought-through sale could ruin a brand.

At Weststar there were sometimes weeks when the park wasn't fully booked. I could easily have panicked and sanctioned bookings for stag and hen parties, even though it was something that went against the core values we had in place. But if I had done so I would have devastated the brand as a family holiday park.

It is easy to fall into the trap of thinking that a company has to get money in at all costs, particularly in an economic downturn when no one really knows what is round the corner, but it is a slippery slope. In Weststar's case, for example, if we had opened the doors to raucous parties it would not have been long before our core customers went elsewhere because at least some of them would have a bad experience, and word does spread fast. After just one bad decision, the people I really wanted to book would quickly turn their backs on us because Weststar was no longer the brand they thought it was.

Taking orders at all costs, even in a downturn, is a short-term strategy. It says that the company does not care about its brand, and a company that takes this approach is doomed to failure. You need your brand to be memorable and sustained, which means that it must communicate its message. People often make the mistake of thinking that branding is just about the logo. What it really is, however, is the language the company and its products speak. It is the way the business behaves and how the products look.

Think of a car, for example. It is not simply a tangible, physical entity that is bought and sold. Deciding on the make and model of a new car is an incredibly complex process for consumers because of what that car will say about them. Nearly everyone forms an opinion about other people based on the car they drive. A blood-red Ferrari? Young, rich City type. A 4×4 Chelsea tractor? Must be an urban mum off on the school run. These assumptions may be wrong, but most people make them, whether or not they admit to it. That car might have great fuel-consumption figures, go from 0 to 60 in just a few seconds and have space in the boot for a small elephant, but what is most important to the majority of buyers is the brand. The brand is that often intangible benefit that makes the product valuable to the consumer and it is the brand that is important.

Once a brand has become established, it becomes like a person. People say the same sort of things about it that they would about someone they know, things like, 'Oh no, I wouldn't go to Waitrose for cut-price, mass-produced food – "they" are not that type of store.' And if a brand does something out of character it brings everyone up short because they think it is a bit odd and don't really like it.

Every time the consumer thinks of a good brand all sorts of emotions should come to mind. Take a hugely successful brand like Innocent Smoothies. First of all the name conjures up a great-tasting product. Then, in my mind's eye, I will visualise its cool packaging covered with clever slogans. Almost without knowing it, I will have thought about the whiz-kids behind the idea who built a massive business from nowhere. That is quite a lot to be packed behind a simple name.

Creating a brand takes time. I would begin by using market research to consider what it is about a product that attracts consumers and build the message around it. Then think of a way to speak to customers about this message so that they will instantly understand and get behind the product. So, for example, if it is a cool and funky product, like the youdoodoll, everything about it should be cool and funky. The language on the packaging and in promotions is snappy and creative, and any new products in the range should follow the same track. Conversely, Prowaste, the construction-waste recycling business, is branded with a mix of business-like, industrial qualities alongside practical, technical images.

For this reason it is important that everything a company does around a brand fits in with the culture that has been created. So, with youdoodoll, for example, it is absolutely right to follow guerrilla-marketing techniques, such as viral videos on the Internet. We have even set up life-size youdoodolls without explanation in public places, such as railway stations and shopping centres, and customers love the quirkiness. However, with a more traditional and seemingly upright brand these stunts would be totally out of place.

Once the brand has been created protect it at all costs and do not let anything else get in the way. I rejected one of the early packaging designs for youdoopets, a brand extension capitalising on the success of youdoodoll, because it did not clearly represent the original brand. The proofs for the new design said: 'Sarah Lu presents youdoodoll's youdoopets, another invention brought to you by youdoodolls.' It was impossible to distinguish the original brand and utterly confusing. The logos might have all looked the same, but there were three different messages. Youdoodoll is the brand that everyone should recognise when they walk into a shop, and that is the only aspect that should be emphasised. Everything else should depend on that.

Customers don't have time to trawl through the words on a box. They learn to love a brand, see it in a shop, make a decision and buy it. But how do you get a customer to fall in love with a brand? Like everything else in business it's not easy, but if you have a plan and are prepared to put in the work, it doesn't have to be complicated.

Where there's a plan there's a way (again)

I have lost count of the number of firms that have said to me, 'We are a marketing-driven business.' What I hope they are actually trying to say is that they have a really good product and that marketing is important to the company because they have to get the message out. That is fine. Marketing on its own means nothing. Without the product it is nothing. The long and short of it is that companies usually don't really know what marketing is. Although there are some clever catchphrases that can be used to define it, most people would have real trouble even describing the difference between sales and marketing.

I would urge any company that is unsure of where to start in marketing – and, as I said, there are many – to begin by writing down on an A4 sheet a definition of their target market. They should ask themselves to define their main customer. Amazingly, many companies are unable to articulate their target market. I find this astonishing. How can a business sell a product or service to someone when they don't know who they are, how they behave, what they think and perhaps, most importantly, where they shop?

Marketing on its own means nothing

I would even go as far as getting a photograph of an imaginary 'perfect' customer, attaching it to that A4 sheet and filling in details about them. It could say something along the lines of: 'This is Charlotte. She is 29 years old; she shops at Sainsbury's, Selfridges and Debenhams; she buys mainly organic goods and Fairtrade products; she reads *Marie Claire* and the *Guardian*; she was educated at Manchester University, where she read history.' It is so much easier to plan a marketing campaign once a company starts to think and talk about their customers as real people. That sheet and photograph should be pinned to the wall of an office, certainly in the early stages of a company's life. Every time a word is written or a brochure planned, I would refer to that sheet and ask myself: 'Is this in a language that Charlotte would understand? Would this inspire her? How will I get her to notice this product?'

After writing a statement of who the customer is, the next stage is to write a complete marketing plan that sets out how the company will reach this target market. This will really help you to think about what you are trying to say, who you are saying it to and, therefore, how you are going to say it. You can find a section on all the elements of the perfect marketing plan at the end of the book.

Once the plan is complete, please, please do not think, 'That's it, I've got that out of the way!' It is an important document, to which you should constantly refer and not leave on a dusty shelf. You will have made some hefty assumptions, some of which will be wrong and need adjusting, and customers change all the time, which means constantly revisiting the plan. In a few years' time 'Charlotte', our imaginary customer, may well be married and have a family. Her priorities will have changed drastically. Is the company 'growing up' with Charlotte, or is it targeting the next generation of Charlottes, who will themselves probably have different tastes and preferences from the previous generation? Is there anything the company can do to hold on to that hard-won customer as she changes and grows up? It may even be a simple case of packaging the offering in a slightly different way to appeal to the new generation. The worst possible action is to put a marker in the sand, declare that the company knows who the core customer is and blindly stick with it whatever happens.

I would recommend that there is an annual formal reappraisal of the marketing document, but ideally it should be something that a company does every day because this will mean that it is aware of its customers' changing needs. This is an important part of the marketing mix. A business should be constantly re-evaluating what it is that its product offers that customers value and whether its appearance or function need to be changed to meet new aspirations. By focusing on what their customers are saying while keeping an eye on the competition, the company will be streets ahead and won't need to do gimmicky, time-wasting things like introducing new products just for the sake of keeping up with their competitors.

If I were at Weststar today I would be regularly walking around the park and watching my customers. I would look at what they are wearing, I would notice that the cars in the car parks have more eco-friendly stickers on them and that the older children are glued to hand-held electronic devices. In fact, even though I left the business in 2006, I would even today still be around 80 per cent right in my summary of holiday-park customer behaviour.

Businesses need to define their customer base and then keep it in mind, no matter what happens. As I have found out, this can be a hard habit to break.

Don't get tangled up in the web

One of the most significant recent developments by far in marketing is the explosion of the Internet. However, too many businesses make the mistake of assuming that all they need to make the sales soar is to have a website. Unsurprisingly, it is a little more complicated than that. Every company, no matter how tiny, should have a presence on the Internet, even if it is a single shop with a one-page site simply saying what is on offer, why a customer should choose to take up that offer and contact details. The ability to capture customers' details is not necessary, although it is an advantage.

Bearing in mind that the letters www in Internet addresses stand for World Wide Web, far too many websites are oddly insular. They ignore the potential worldwide audience and talk about themselves in a way that is neither pertinent nor relevant and that limits their customer range to their immediate locality. They don't think about the wider audience and how they will be reading the site, and they make far too many assumptions about potential customers. When they are designing a website companies shouldn't just think about their existing customers; they should think about who could be their customers. They should take the geographical barriers down that they themselves have built up and expand their trading horizons.

Build an *effective* online presence

Entrepreneurs are generally quite vain, thinking that people really care about their story. I know that if I look on the website of any potential early stage investment there will probably be a prominent 'my story' section. But if I am trying to book a bio-diesel vehicle or buy a kitchen gadget, I honestly don't care about the founders' struggle to get the product to the market or how they came up with the idea while tending their allotment one day. I don't want people to sit around browsing my website out of interest. I want people to buy my products. That is what a website is generally supposed to do. If 'my story' does not add anything to the decision to buy it might, in fact, divert people away from it because a customer who was initially interested might get bored after trawling through 1,000 words of rags-to-riches prose.

Internet marketing – backed up by sales – is a great opportunity to get a company known around the world, but it is a completely different proposition from using traditional media. It is unlikely that a start-up or small business has the technical know-how in-house to design and build their own website from scratch. I have come across far too many small businesses that have tried to do this in an effort to save money. At the same time, without batting an eyelid, they are only too happy to continue placing the advertisement in the local paper that is producing next to no revenue.

I would always use external experts to design or advise on website design. Also, I think it is disastrous for a business to try and build its own website unless, of course, building websites is their business or they have previously worked with websites and have the technical skill. It is a highly specialised area. There is a real danger that it will look as if they have designed it themselves and don't really know what they are doing. I know how websites should be built, but I would not dream of trying to build one on my own. In addition, as well as getting a professional job, it is helpful to get an outsider to look at it with a fresh pair of eyes to decide whether it is hitting the spot and providing would-be customers with the details they actually care about.

So, what are the key factors to remember when a company is designing a decent website? First, the only page that people are guaranteed to see if they find the site is the front page. If that looks wrong or if people are confused or disappointed by that page, they will go no further and will leave the site. If a company tries to be too clever on an opening page or starts off with a complicated introduction, one of two things will happen: the consumer will get utterly confused and think that this is not the website they had hoped it was, or, worse still, it will take ages to load up and the person who is left with the spinning wheel of doom at the other end will simply click elsewhere and never even see the swanky site at all.

A business should put itself in a potential customer's shoes. What would they expect to land on and see? What is it that they are looking for? The front page has to represent the product, summarising its qualities and listing reasons to buy it. It should be as simple as possible and, if it is a one-product business, there should be a prominent 'buy me' button on the front page so that the customer doesn't have to go any further. It is, after all, all about making it easy for the customer to buy the product and certainly not about putting any barriers in the way.

I was once asked by a friend to do some work with a well-known online organic food delivery company. Their marketing person had left, and I was asked to cast an eye over the company's website. The moment I opened the page I could see they had a problem with delivery times and appeared to be experiencing resistance from customers to signing up because they didn't get the time they wanted. How did I know this? There it was on the landing page in black and white: 'Check your delivery times.' Now, as a prospective customer I would not have decided if I wanted to buy from this company yet. I may not even be entirely sure what they sell. But, I would immediately be anxious about potential problems with delivery slots. The company had clearly not viewed the website from the customers' point of view and thought it helpful to highlight the delivery issue on the front page.

Part of making it easy to buy a product is to provide easy-to-find contact details and a telephone number for customers to ring if they feel the need to talk to a human. Some people still have a residual nervousness about buying on the Internet, and it gives an added layer of comfort to consumers to know that there is a person at the end of the line.

One thing that I absolutely would not include in the design is hundreds of click-on links to other pages on the web, unless, of course, you plan to make your money through advertising. If a website offers an easy route for visitors to read this page here or that interview there, what it is actually doing is asking their hard-won visitors to leave their website. I worked with one company that sent visitors off to magazine and newspaper websites to read articles about their product, and all too often the same articles listed contact details and reviews of less expensive competitors. Apart from that glaring error, if people are directed to another publication it is too easy to be distracted. Suddenly the browser will read another story, and that will take them on to another, and before they know it they will be dozens of pages away from where they first started, probably never to return.

The design of the website should not include everything the company can possibly feature on a page. People trawling the net have a short attention span, and the more buttons, click-throughs and links there are, the more confused they will become. Firms shouldn't get carried away with comparing themselves to competitors' sites and thinking, well, they have 12 buttons, so I need 12 buttons too. What is it that the company actually wants to tell potential customers? It is not a question of whether it looks whizz-bang and lovely. What is more important is what job it is doing. If the website is selling, make it easy to buy.

How the site should look is down to gut instinct and design flair. Some products do go with certain colours – for example, a technological company, providing something like machine parts, would probably favour black, greys and greens, while an environmental company is more likely to go down the route of greens, blues and yellows. If the site is selling a product for £99, then it should look as if it is selling a product for £99 and not be so chic and exclusive that it might scare off budget-conscious customers. A good way to test it is to ask people to look at the site after taking off the brand names and main copy. If they can't guess the type of product that's for sale or which sector it is in, it could be time to go back to the drawing board.

Put yourself out there

In the promotions part of the marketing mix original thought should come into its own. Unfortunately, when the subject of promotion is raised, people usually assume that it just means a bit of public relations (PR). There is an extraordinary assumption that a press release will cover the tricky task of reaching existing and potential customers.

Even if it were just a matter of a 'bit of PR' most companies don't spend nearly enough time planning their publicity campaigns. There is so much more to PR than scribbling down a press release. It is about understanding who is influential in particular areas, building relationships with the media and key opinion formers, and keeping in constant touch even if there is nothing company-specific to say.

At Weststar we had contact sheets detailing the main media contacts, and we would regularly remind the team to keep in touch. Even if it was a call to say, 'Have you heard anything? I've heard this . . .', it kept the conversation going. Then, when we actually needed to pass something on, the busy journalist on the end of the line wouldn't be thinking, 'Why is this business phoning me?'

I would also be constantly aware of what was going on in the wider environment by watching and listening to the news. I remember a campaign in the 1990s in which Hoover offered a free holiday for every Hoover vacuum cleaner bought. The campaign, perhaps not surprisingly, was an overnight sensation and became so successful that it became an administrative nightmare. The chosen airline simply could not cope with the demand and was unable to provide the flights that Hoover had promised as part of the sales promotion. It was not long before the press caught on, and pretty soon news of the growing fiasco was on every front page. Within days of the first bit of bad press going to print, Weststar had a campaign up and running that turned the whole problem on its head. Piggybacking the huge media exposure and public interest we ran a campaign saying: 'Book a Weststar holiday within a specified period and get a free Hoover.' The results were phenomenal. Not only did we sell a huge number of holidays as a direct result of the campaign, but the media exposure was so great that bookings for other periods outside of the offer began to flood in.

At Weststar every time there was a story about airport chaos our marketing machine would counteract it by stressing how much easier it was to avoid airport queues altogether and travel in your own time. If I had still been there at the time of the disastrous opening of Heathrow's Terminal 5 I would have been on to it straight away. Our advertising rate would have shot up as we extolled the virtues of calm, relaxed and beautifully organised British seaside holidays. In marketing a business has to be constantly aware of what is going on and when the right moment arises for a burst of targeted activity.

I would avoid at all costs trusting in that old favourite 'any publicity is good publicity' mantra. It is simply not true. I am asked to do press interviews all the time, but apart from not having enough hours in the day, the first thing I always ask myself is: 'Why am I doing this? What is my message?' There is absolutely no point sitting in front of a camera or microphone and spouting on about myself. I am a businessperson, not a publicity-seeking celebrity. How does this interview help my investments or my community? If any of the companies I invest in agree to interviews, I always ask them to write down three messages that they want to get out there and make sure that they do. It staggers me when companies get valuable media time and then spectacularly fail to even mention their product or company name. They should be controlling the situation.

Once again, entrepreneurs should not get so bogged down in the detail of how they invented the product, what it was made of and where they sourced the material. Forget that. Instead, try to think what it is that a customer would want to know and gear all your answers towards telling them something that will make them at least want to find out more about, and hopefully even buy, your product.

Sadly, I often see an equally chaotic approach to advertising campaigns. There is a propensity for small businesses to think of advertising in traditional terms, such as simply placing an advertisement in a local newspaper or producing a few fliers. There are, however, many alternative and more imaginative ways of advertising.

Before planning a campaign, I would ask the following questions: Do I have enough people coming through the door? If I need more people, how am I going to get them and where am I going to find them? What do they do all day? Then I would decide the best route to speak to the customer. If they are at work, for example, why not call up that workplace and ask if it is all right to put up a poster in the canteen? Alternatively, why not take a product into the local community or offices and offer a free sample, saying 'try something different on me'. It is not a waste of time and can certainly be more effective than traditional advertising.

Timing is critical, too. If, for example, a business is marketing to low-income families there is no point advertising to them near the end of the month, a week before their pay packet is due. There are too many other pressures on their already dwindling resources. Make contact in the first week of the month when they actually have some money.

Similarly, if a business is conducting an online campaign there is little point in sending out marketing emails to office workers late on a Friday afternoon because the recipients will inevitably be completely unreceptive. An e-shot should coincide with customer behaviour.

I have a golden rule on advertising. Never, ever respond to a cold call selling a last-minute slot in a local paper or a heavily discounted page in a glossy magazine. A business should make its own decisions about the timing of an advertising campaign based on the carefully thought-out marketing plan. If the business needed an advertising slot, it should have identified that it needed it when it wrote the marketing plan, and it should not be waiting for somebody to tell it over the telephone that it needs one. A company that blindly buys into these advertising cold calls is dancing to the media company's tune. A business should always be composing its own tune and be in complete control of what it does and doesn't need.

'Lunch is for wimps'

I don't normally eat lunch out of choice, but I do make time to have some lunches with my team because they can be extremely useful. I don't think everybody has to get together, have a glass of wine and slap each other on the back. However, lunches with a purpose are a good environment to talk about key issues. In my experience putting people around a dinner table will always produce some interesting angles that previously may not have been considered. Everyone is used to having dinner in a social setting where it is the norm to search for a new topic and some common ground with fellow diners. There is a far more random, circular thought process than in a corporate setting, and even the shape and intimacy of the table can change the direction of the conversation. Put that same group in the meeting room back at the office, tell them that they are there to discuss next year's capital expenditure budget and the conversation will follow a completely different tack. Their guard will be up, they will be watching what they say, and the focus of the debate will narrow considerably.

Chapter 9
Building your sales

Most businesses I have worked with in the past have misunderstood the sales and marketing process. Remarkably, after everything that entrepreneurs go through to bring a product to market they often seem to think that their brainchild will sell itself, which is just nonsense – potential purchasers need a reason, and a good reason at that, to buy the product. Another mistake is to say 'yes' to any offer that comes along without thinking about what they are trying to achieve. When it comes to sales, I am frequently amazed how little time people spend on them. There they are, having gone to all the trouble of setting up a business whose whole purpose is to sell a product or service, and how much time do they spend actually getting sales? Barely any, is the answer. When I compare it to the hours entrepreneurs devote to getting their office just so, I could weep.

I am not sure what is behind this reticence. I sometimes wonder if it is the reputation salespeople have. You know the ones I mean. I have seen many people who have bragged that they are really good salesmen because they can sell any product. The phrase 'I could sell ice to the Eskimos' comes to mind, but that is a real turn-off as far as I'm concerned. I won't employ these super-salesmen. It's clear that they have no real passion, that they don't care what they are selling and that they don't have the slightest interest in anything but themselves. I am always alert to people who try to sell me stuff they don't care about, don't know about or, even worse, don't particularly like.

I am not alone in this. The public are much more switched on and sophisticated these days, and we've come a long way from the days when we used to accept the smooth patter of a snake-oil salesman who would bombard the crowds with lies until they gave in and bought his wares. The modern consumer is much more knowledgeable about what they want, and if they do get sold the wrong thing they are going to know it. When this happens not only have you lost that customer's trust, but you've also lost the trust of everybody else they tell of their bad experience. This is particularly true in difficult economic times when cash becomes ever more precious and customers are looking for good value.

Selling is all about getting a customer to believe in the product. And who could be more convincing than the founder of the company? It's true that entrepreneurs have a lot on their plate when they are starting up a business, but they don't want to fall into the trap of becoming, to borrow an expression from my good friend and Dragon colleague Theo Paphitis, a 'busy fool'. There are too many would-be entrepreneurs who fail to understand that rushing around and working hard all day is not enough to make a successful business. Doing everything themselves, from the

Nothing sells itself

bookkeeping to designing their own website, does not mean everything is going to work out fine. It won't. You have to be intelligent about the things you put your effort into, and sales should be one of the top priorities.

All good sales begin with a well-positioned product

Most of the hard work required for sales should have been done in the development stage. It tickles me pink when people come on *Dragons' Den* and talk winsomely about how they would really like to benefit from the sales and marketing experience of the Dragons. Generally it means they have a product, they may even have a patent, but somehow they have never considered how they might sell the wretched thing. Every time you take a decision about a new product, from the colour it's going to be to the sort of packaging it will have, you should be keeping your target market in mind.

One of the most basic mistakes that entrepreneurs make is in pricing their product. They range from pitching it way too low, like Max McMurdo of reestore, who was working from a completely unrealistic cost price, to aiming way too high, like Nick Nethercott with his high-tech coffee tables. Getting the pricing right is one of the most important factors in selling. No one can be persuaded to buy a product unless they are prepared to pay the price for it. Many people would love a Ferrari, but most won't buy one because they can't afford it.

Being plugged into your target market will really help you deal with potentially tricky issues, such as pricing. My main aim in pricing is to find a level that represents the best value. That might also mean that the product is the most expensive, but if it is so much better than everybody else's and lasts three times as long it will represent better value. Remember, value isn't necessarily financial. It is whatever importance the customer invests in that product. It might be that the product lasts longer, smells better or tastes nicer, and the customer's perception will depend on where their priorities lie. To steal a march on its competitors a business has to understand the basis on which customers are valuing a product and aim to be the best in that area.

For example, one of the most memorable long-running campaigns that successfully promoted the value of a product, rather than the price, was the one for Fairy washing-up liquid, which found a variety of innovative ways to show that the product lasted '50 per cent longer than the next best-selling brand'. To drive home the message, the company even set up a PR stunt where one bottle of Fairy Liquid washed a record-breaking 14,763 dirty plates.

During an economic downturn, being tuned into the market is more important than ever. There are opportunities, but the whole business model has to fit in with an environment in which people are feeling nervous and are being careful with their money. Products don't have to be 'cheap', but they do need to be seen as being good value. That means that businesses will have to change the language they use to communicate with their customers and the way they package a product so that it offers value for money,

Value is the main consideration in pricing

or can even be seen as a good-value, luxury treat for hard-pressed consumers.

Price can be something of a blunt instrument, but it is also a good barometer. For example, if a business has more customers than it can physically handle, it might be a sign it is underpricing the product. If that is the case the company needs to do something about it, because otherwise it might not be able adequately to service all of its customers and might even be in danger of losing them altogether. It is important to establish quickly what the market will take. There is no point making something everybody wants if it is too expensive and they refuse to pay the price.

There are, of course, hard and fast rules about pricing from a retail point of view, and each sector will have a sector norm or standard mark-up on their cost price. However, even if the margins clearly show that a particular product should sell at £10.25, if entrepreneurs think it will sell twice as many for £9.99 they should listen to their instinct. Businessmen who just do a flat multiplier of how much it costs to manufacture a product, plus costs, plus retail mark-up, are behaving like calculators. Entrepreneurs should listen and adjust to the market. They will think, 'I can do better with this,' or they will say to themselves that the margin says 100 per cent, but I might take 80 per cent and sell a lot more of them. That is what sets them apart from the also-rans.

At the other end of the pricing spectrum, turning out to be a little 'toppy' on price is not a disaster. If a customer says the product is lovely but too expensive, businesses should make sure they record their details. Then they have a great excuse to go back to them if they do decide to drop the price. My philosophy would be to start towards the top end of the price range – not ridiculously high but in a reasonable way – test the market and see. Once a price has been set it is difficult to raise it without upsetting the customers, but it looks great to offer a keener price to good customers.

I am often asked if it is worth offering both a low-cost and a premium version of a product to increase the reach of the overall market. My answer is 'yes', but it has to be done skilfully because it is still vital that products at both ends of the scale share the same values. Tesco, for example, can get away with having premium and economy lines because the brand has a firmly entrenched set of values.

The safest strategy is to develop one brand and establish it in the market before hanging new sub-brands off the original. When new products are developed at different price points the company must make sure that they still share the same brand priorities as the original, such as being well made or fun or ethical or whatever it may be. A good strong brand should be able to withstand a considerable amount of sub-activity.

Get out there and sell!

Once you have developed your winning product there really is nothing for it but to get out there and draw people's attention to it. If you have got it right, selling your product should simply be a matter of putting it in front of the right people and proving that it is as saleable as you think it is.

I often get the impression from my investments that one of the main reasons they are thrilled to have me on board is because they now have access to my industry contacts and expect them to ease the sales and marketing process considerably. Those who are brave – or ill-advised – enough to voice this view are put straight pretty smartly. Yes, I can get a business in front of some pretty powerful people, but if the business is not absolutely right and ready for it, it will be an embarrassing waste of everyone's time. At a stroke, that business would lose all further opportunities with this contact because it would never be able to go back to that person. No, my investment is not an easy route to circumnavigate the hard work of sales and marketing.

Selling a product is not complicated or scary as long as it is a product that enough people actually want or, even better, need. For example, one of the easiest strategies, particularly if it is a low-cost manufactured product, is simply sending out samples. Go on the Internet, find the top ten potential customers, call them up, find out the name of the buyers and send them one. If it is not possible to find out the name of a buyer, address it to 'the product buyer'. Enclose a letter with the product explaining why they should buy it, when it is available and how much it will cost. The next step – and this is really key – is to follow up on all of those initial letters. People do need to be given time to make a decision, but I don't think it pays to be passive. Ask for feedback. Ask if you're getting the service right. You can even ask if you can contact them again after a week. Just make sure you keep the lines of communication open.

Sell them something they want and they will come back for more

It works. It really works. People always say to me that it is difficult to speak to a buyer, and yes, it is difficult, but don't forget that a buyer's job is to buy products. They may need a bit of chasing, and they may even need a bit of persuasion, but it's part of their job to be on the lookout for great products, and if your product is right for them you should be able to strike a deal. Even if the product isn't right for them, it's important to ask them why so that you can refine and improve. Selling can be as simple as this.

Over the years I have gained a reputation for being good at sales and marketing. I am good, but that is not my sole area of expertise. I am a business generalist, with a good eye for sales and marketing, but I do know my limitations. One of my strengths is being able to spot what can be done for a business, and that sometimes means bringing in a specialist. In the case of LateralCorp, the fashion import business, for instance, I have enlisted the services of Exposure, a specialist marketing house for the fashion industry, for the simple reason that I could spend forever trying to make the contacts Exposure already has. I've got loads of contacts, but I don't know everybody in an industry. Why would I think that I could do a better job than a company that specialises in the fashion industry?

Too many companies rely on the fact that they have a sales and marketing department and think that that department can deal with any topic that comes under the heading sales and marketing. It can't. There are many, many specialist topics within sales and marketing, and sometimes you should not be afraid to call in the experts.

But be prepared for setbacks

Perhaps entrepreneurs shy away from putting any effort into sales because they don't want to hear that the product they've put their all into is no good. Let's face it, they are almost certain to hear the odd bad thing about their product, but it's silly to let their pride get in the way. Successful entrepreneurs will not sit back and think, 'Oh well, you can't win them all.' They will ask the awkward questions, get the feedback and use that information to adapt and improve.

And it's not just in the early stages of selling a product that you will be getting knock-backs. Even established companies receive rejections and customer complaints, and I do believe that how they cope with them is a mark of success. Take customer complaints, for example. I don't agree with the old cliché that 'the customer is always right', largely because I think that the issue of right or wrong when it comes to customers is irrelevant. The customer is the customer. If companies want to keep customers they had better find out what it is they have to do to make those customers feel wanted and happy. Judging whether they are right or wrong to complain is really not the point.

Complaints are actually a huge opportunity. If the company sorts one out the newly satisfied customer will undoubtedly tell everyone how their complaint was quickly resolved and how absolutely brilliant the firm is. I'm always amazed when I see a member of staff waving a copy of the terms and conditions in the face of an obviously fed-up customer. How is that going to resolve anything? There are much better ways to deal with a complaint. In my experience the best customers have come back to a business

Customer complaints are an opportunity

as a result of an initial problem. When someone complains it opens up a relationship with the company. They are no longer like the casual punter who comes in, buys a drink and then goes home. No, now they have an emotional connection, they feel something about the company that mucked them about. It is up to the company that has sparked that emotion to turn it from something negative into something positive. If that business can turn that customer round and impress them in a personal way, that customer will be an ambassador for the company like no other.

Everybody gets something wrong. If a company is not receiving any complaints, it does not have an adequate complaints procedure. Complaints are customer feedback, and if a company is not seeing any I would be worried indeed that I was missing something.

We had a low complaint rate at Weststar, but that does not mean that we didn't have any complaints at all. We had more than 200,000 people coming through our doors most seasons, and, believe me, we managed to get it wrong for some of them. However, the real issue was the way their complaints were resolved and how quickly. If a complaint ever escalated it was, as far as I was concerned, our fault. It meant that somewhere along the line we had made a wrong decision because that customer came in with a problem and was not satisfied with the result. Whatever the facts of the case, this issue is now entirely our fault and we will get what we deserve.

I would always recommend putting in stringent rules about how complaints should be dealt with, but give enough autonomy to the person facing the customer to put things right. As soon as a complaint is received, the first thing that any member of staff should do is try to resolve the problem. Forget about logging it in the complaints book, trying to find someone senior to pass it on to or passing it on to the 'right' department. No, the person who received the complaint should try to resolve it there and then. If they can do this, and in most cases they should be able to, no one will have to deal with it later.

After taking all possible steps to resolve the complaint, the person who is dealing with it should give the disgruntled customer their name, which will immediately make the customer feel reassured that the matter is being taken seriously and that they have someone they can talk to who understands. It will also help to make sure that the person who is dealing with the complaint feels more responsible. The usual exchange will then go something along the lines of: this is what is going to happen next; if that doesn't happen as it should, this is my name and telephone number. Customers must be left in no doubt that their concerns are being addressed.

Next, and this is key, log all the details of the customer complaint. If this does not happen, when the customer returns and the original contact point is out of the office, the customer will have to explain the whole story all over again, and you can be certain that that is really going to wind them up. The problem annoyed them enough in the first place; now, after being made all these promises, they are back to square one. How do you think that is going to make them feel? At Weststar I always made sure that we had a rigid set of processes so that everyone knew what customers were talking about when they got back in touch following a complaint. If I had calls put through to me at my Exeter office I would immediately say, 'Yes, the general manager has talked to me about this.' That simple act of recognition would usually diffuse the situation immediately because the customer would be left with the impression that the issue mattered enough to the company for senior management to discuss the problem. By then, all being well, I would be well on the way to securing a loyal customer for life.

I probably learned this lesson back in my days running a bingo concession. I've always been lucky in that I have a good memory for faces, and I would always say, 'Hello again. How are you?' to people who had returned to the holiday park for the second or third time. It delighted them and immediately put them at ease.

Look at it from their point of view. There they are, in a strange environment where they don't really know anybody, and somebody has remembered that they have been there before. That simple act of recognition made them feel as if they had come home. The minute I said 'Hello again' I made sure that the bingo hall became the centre of their holiday. If they were ever wondering what they should do next, they'd say, 'Let's go and see Deborah at the bingo.' They were not really going simply for the game; they were going to sit somewhere with people they felt comfortable with. If it was quiet and the pace of the game needed to be slower, I would use the microphone to chat with my 'friends'. Never underestimate the power of speaking to somebody over a microphone. There could be hundreds of people around, but I would look at that one person and single them out. Priceless.

Too many companies hide from complaints and try to avoid confrontation by dealing with them through email and letters. That does not form relationships. A business should look as if it takes any complaints against it personally and should feel like that, too. I would want anyone who was unhappy with a Weststar holiday to know that it personally bothered me that they did not have a good holiday with us – and it did.

A bird in the hand ...

I am often astounded by the number of companies that seem to be prepared to ignore the customers they have in order to go after new ones. Look at the mortgage market, for example. In the boom days before the credit crunch people were switching mortgages left, right and centre. Banks would flatly refuse to budge when people were offered a better rate elsewhere, so the customer would switch and six months later the bank would be in touch offering a discount rate to win them back. It was crazy. It is always well worth spending money on keeping hard-earned customers happy.

Customers who have shopped with a company before no longer need to be told about the business and its products. If anything, it is a little insulting to do so. If, say, they have taken ten holidays with a firm they already know there is an indoor pool because they will have swum in it dozens of times. They will look at the marketing material aghast, asking themselves: 'Why are they telling me this as if I have never been there?' What is required here is a subtle move into relationship marketing. This is all about

Keep existing customers happy

making a customer feel good about their relationship with the company and creating an environment that makes it difficult for them to decide to leave and shop elsewhere.

At Weststar we divided up our database and devised campaigns that were specifically targeted at the people who had been with us for one, two or three years. We even went back to customers who had stayed with us ten years before and who had grown up and had young children of their own. The message was all about what was new since their last visit, but it was couched in a language that made them proud to be recognised as a loyal customer. So we would say things like, 'We haven't seen you for a while' or 'Since you were with us last . . .'. We would also recognise that they had some knowledge of our product with phrases such as 'You will have seen this' or 'Of course, you will already know about that.' Once that long-term relationship is forged and acknowledged, there is a relationship from which it is hard for them to walk away.

It is worth paying attention to relationship marketing because it costs less to retain a customer than it does to acquire one. It is a huge mistake to spend considerable time and money on acquiring customers and then upset them by virtually ignoring them thereafter. Once customers decide to walk away, they are expensive to get back because the company also has to address the issue of why they made up their mind to go in the first place and persuade them that the company has changed. It's also necessary to decide if it's worth investing money to get them back, when frankly this should never have become an issue.

To concentrate the mind it is a good idea to make a simple calculation of the lifetime value of a customer. First of all, it is important to establish the size of the potential market and then set targets to gain a sensible portion of that market. Let's say, for simplicity, that the potential market size is £500,000 and the business in question intends to win £100,000 of that new spend in year one with a product that costs £10. We can see that we need to attract 10,000 new customers. So, how much should the business be prepared to spend acquiring each customer? Well, the answer depends entirely on the expected behaviour of that customer. If I expect the customer to stay with me for one year, then it is clearly nonsense to spend £10 to acquire that customer. If, on the other hand, prior customer knowledge tells me that customers are likely to stay with me for an average of five years, buying one product a year, it is reasonable to allocate £10 to acquire them. Yes, the company will lose money in year one, but by the time it gets to year five the percentage acquisition cost will be negligible. The cost of retention is nowhere near that of acquisition, but it makes sense to devote, say, £1 a year in the budget to keeping those customers sweet.

This is not a difficult calculation to make, but it could prove fruitful.

Marketing is an odd discipline. Companies often declare that it is the answer to everything, but when times get difficult it is the first thing they cut in their budgets. The reasoning behind this is, I suppose, that it is not always easy to see the immediate effect of a marketing strategy. It is not as clear-cut as saying 'I will buy this for X and sell it for Y and there is my profit of Z.' However, I would say that an economic downturn is one of the most effective times to ramp up a marketing campaign – media space will certainly be less expensive, after all. There is a clear opportunity to make a bigger impact with less of a financial commitment at a time when everyone else is cutting back.

There are many misapprehensions about sales and marketing, but it really couldn't be simpler: a company has a product, it tells everyone that it has it, it gives them a reason to buy, then it delivers and keeps on delivering.

Taking the online route

In some ways the Internet has made things much easier for entrepreneurs. If you have a brand-new product and want to bring it to market you can just design a website and start selling direct to customers. Of course, because it is so easy to get on the web there are a lot of sites out there, so the trick is to make sure that customers can not only find your site, but also buy the product there easily and efficiently. Ideally, when potential customers visit a company's website they should come away with the feeling that they have found exactly what, if not more than, they wanted.

In series six of *Dragons' Den* Theo Paphitis and I invested in Magic Whiteboard, a product that allows the user to combine the best of a flip chart and a whiteboard in seconds. It is a roll of sheets that stick to any hard surface using static. Each 20 metre roll contains 25 perforated sheets, and these can be reused at least 20 times. It is a great product, and the entrepreneurs, Neil and Laura Westwood, had done a fair job with the original design of their website, but we could see immediately that we needed to revamp it.

Designing a website is all about balancing the sometimes competing demands of web design and web optimisation. Magic Whiteboard was a business product, but the site lacked professional appeal. It had too much text, it wasn't pushing the sales opportunity hard enough, and when would-be buyers were fed through to the shopping cart, the branding disappeared, leaving them with the unhappy and uneasy sensation that they had 'left' the website.

We could see immediately what we needed to do. The first step was to remedy the shopping cart branding. Buyers should feel completely secure when buying online. The process should be seamless, with as few steps as possible to place an order. With regard to the design, it needs to be eye-catching and clever, but websites also need to have the right amount of information, not only for the customer but also for search engines. The golden rule is give customers key information and selling points up front and then, if they need more details, point them in the right direction to find them. So we stripped back the home page to give it a clearer message and set the tone to gear site visitors towards buying. If someone has typed in the URL or found the site on Google, they are already ready to order and it's the website's job to help them do that. Internet selling is not the place to be humble. 'Let us tell you all about Magic Whiteboard because it's so great, oh and perhaps you might want to order,' is a waste of time.

There are plenty of consultants who work in this area, and I would really recommend spending the money to get the website

Make sure your website delivers

right and then to track its progress. You will need to see all the statistics on the site's performance, from how many visitors there have been, to how many return visitors there are, to how long they stay, and which page they are leaving at. If people are landing on the site and bouncing straight off, the site is clearly not what they thought it was, and the key terms on the front page are probably wrong. Alternatively, if people are spending a long time on the site but not buying, this might be because the website has become too complicated or because there is too much information. If there are a large number of return visitors, however, it clearly means that they like what they see. Run that against a sales conversion rate – that is, the number of people who visited the site against the number who actually bought something – and an in-depth picture of how effective the site is will begin to emerge. It is possible to work out why people don't buy a product with the help of detailed statistics of when and where most of them are leaving the site.

One other note of caution. Always keep an eye on competitors and whether they are trying to muscle in on the success of an Internet operation. The beauty – and the danger – of the Internet is that this is not a hard thing to do. Following Magic Whiteboard's success on the *Den* and its subsequent high sales, both online and in retailers, several imitators have tried to cash in on the idea. Instead of selling the roll, which retails at £25, these copycats were selling single sheets for £4.95 on the Internet. Needless to say, both I and Magic Whiteboard's founders were straight on to Google to remedy the situation. Search engines will not allow 'passing off' – the practice of copying a product and pretending the two are linked – and it is a good idea for any company to monitor any suspicious sales of their products.

If your website is doing its job and pulling in orders, you might find yourself in the enviable position of not having time to fill those orders. Rather than get behind, I would recommend investigating the possibility of employing a fulfilment house. These operations take all the orders and man the telephone calls, while all a business has to do is give them the price list and product. It is probably not feasible for a highly technical product, because the order-takers at a fulfilment house cannot be expected to have the in-depth specialist knowledge they will need to answer potential customers' queries, but it is perfect for a simple retail proposition, such as the youdoodoll. Customers don't need to be told anything more about the doll: they can see a picture of it on the Internet, press the 'buy' button and the order goes straight to the fulfilment house where it is picked, packed and dispatched immediately.

There are plenty of fulfilment houses, and a quick trawl of the Internet should show the main ones. I would start by looking for companies that deal in products that are similar to your own, not only because they will be used to the peculiarities that may be involved, but also because they may be willing to introduce your product to their existing contacts to build up their business as well as yours.

Selling in a downturn

Whether it is online or by way of a retail outlet, the key to selling any product has to be making it easy for customers to buy it. This is more important than ever before as people watch every penny they spend.

If businesses have not already done so, they should think about where people buy their products and whether, under the circumstances, there might be other forums or opportunities for selling those products. I was recently contacted by a bridal business that has survived for three years but is now barely ticking over in the face of the recession, and the owner was worried that she might have to shut up shop for good. I advised her to start off by asking herself some pertinent questions. Are fewer people going to be getting married post credit crunch or are they simply going to be spending less money on their weddings? I suspect that the number of people getting married will not fall significantly but that those who do will want to spend less and will want better value.

To boost the bottom line this shop owner needs to think creatively about sales. She should look at her current range and make sure it hits the mark. Then she should think about how she could add value. In her case, one quite low-cost and effective way to do this would be by joining forces with other wedding service suppliers who will inevitably be in the same boat and suffering in the downturn. Together they could create offers such as 'Spend £xx and get the wedding cake for free,' or they could club together and come up with a discount or value offers. If they get together the individual companies involved in the promotion will not take a big hit financially, but the customer will get a substantial discount.

Sales is all about making sure that the customer is satisfied that they have got a good purchase and that they have got the value that they wanted out of that purchase. In the current economic conditions people are going to feel cheated if they believe they have been 'talked into' a sale and then not given something of good value. Whatever their notion of value is, they like to think they are getting the best.

If they are to succeed businesses need to satisfy their customers' value systems and not lie to them. Loyal customers have always been important, but now they are truly worth their weight in gold.

Good salespeople listen as much as they talk. They should constantly reappraise how they sell and who they are selling to, and they should adapt to new environments. Everything is fluid today, and the accepted rules of businesses have changed. Anyone who has just one way of selling will be in real trouble.

'You can't turn around a tanker with a speedboat change'

The cliché 'you can't turn around a tanker with a speedboat change' usually comes up when I want to communicate something through the organisation quickly and get an instant reaction. It is the type of expression that is trotted out by executives who shake their heads and whistle through their teeth that this or that action is impossible to get done in that time frame because so many extra factors need to be taken into account. I hate that.

Big businesses should always remember that they are small businesses, but bigger. There should be no problems with communication down the line. Even if an entrepreneur grows their business to employ 10,000 people, they should structure their company so that they can immediately filter their thoughts to every one of those 10,000 people. It is possible. Look at retail giant Tesco, which employs 440,000 staff worldwide in more than 3,700 stores. A great deal of its success is down to its flat structure, which has only six levels between the person at the checkout and the man at the top. If the chief executive, Sir Terry Leahy, makes a decision about strategy it can be communicated around the firm with a speed that would make many smaller firms envious.

My advice to any start-up would be to put its lines of communication in place from the outset. If they do that it will be second nature as the business grows and there is so much more information to absorb and convey to the rest of the team.

Chapter 10
What if I fail?

My first business was a financial failure. When I was 19 years old, fresh out of business school and after a brief stint as a fashion showroom model, I moved to Italy. I wasn't quite sure what I wanted to do – I just had a burning desire to run my own show. I have always loved art and sculpture and could not fail to have been inspired by what I saw during my time in Florence. The craftsmanship, style and breathtaking beauty of what was on offer moved me to make the decision to set up a glass and ceramics import business.

The next few months were a heady mix of dashing around the Italian countryside to visit factories where the air was filled with an intoxicating mix of rich tobacco smoke and chemicals, followed by endless sunny days stumbling down cobbled streets in historic cities to negotiate with immaculately turned-out businessmen and women. Eventually I secured sole-agency distribution rights with a good number of Italian businesses and immediately set about organising the next stage of my plan. I decided to launch my exciting new venture by exhibiting my prizes at the prestigious Top Drawer retail gift fair in London. On my trip back to the UK I was strangely nervous and apprehensive. I wondered if I had my timing right and whether the British public would be ready to recognise the extraordinary style of these Italian works and, more importantly, welcome them into their homes.

As it turned out, my fears were groundless. The reaction was electric and leading stores were soon vying to sell complete ranges of my goods. It was an exhilarating time. I was delighted with my success and quickly imagined that I would be able to grow the business to include works from other European countries.

Then, after a great start, the orders suddenly stopped coming in. At first I simply could not understand what had gone wrong. A quick trawl through top London stores showed there was still a huge public appetite for these goods, but it did not take me long to discover what had happened to my previously thriving business. All my major customers had spotted that there was a huge demand for Italian glass and ceramics, and they had simply cut out the middle man, or in my case woman, and gone to my suppliers to buy the goods direct.

I was forced to think on my feet. Although I had contracts saying that I was the sole agent for these various companies, I quickly realised that to enforce my rights I would probably have to spend at least a year in complex and expensive legal battles, and whatever the final outcome I would have fallen out with my Italian companies and the buyers at the key stores. Either way, my fledgling business was dead in the water.

I am not a sentimental person when it comes to business. My head has always led my heart, and once I have made up my mind about something it doesn't weigh me down. I calculated the odds and saw no point in wasting a year of my time, energy and money on a fight I could never win. So I shut down the company.

The circumstances vary, but hundreds of thousands of entrepreneurs experience business failure every year. The difference between me and the majority who find themselves in trouble and then keep going until the bitter end is that at the moment when I could have got myself into debt and there was a likelihood that it could have got worse, I took the difficult decision to close the business down. Is it good that I had that experience early on in my business career? Yes and no. It was a shock, but even though I was relatively young and inexperienced, I could see what had to be done and I got on with it. I guess I must be that type of person, and, whether it had been then or later, I would probably have reacted in the same way. I have always been brutally honest with myself and with people around me. People can either deal with that or they can't.

Business failure is, of course, a pertinent subject during the current market downturn, and many small businesses are going to the wall every week. However, my argument would be that external factors, including the recession, should not be the major cause of failure in well-run businesses because these factors should come as no big surprise. In the current downturn, which began in 2007, it had been obvious for some time that the market was overheating and there were too many crazy deals going on. A business leader should have understood that and realised that they needed to take action to protect the company from the recession by introducing measures to mitigate against, for example, late-paying customers.

The smaller a business, the better chance it has of kicking against the natural economic cycle. It does, after all, only want a small slice of what is usually a big pie. Being unique and personal makes it much easier to buck a trend. If a business commands the majority of a market it is much more difficult to withstand the trends because it is then dealing with changes in the behaviour of the whole nation.

The most vulnerable businesses in a recession are those that do not stay in touch with their customers and embrace changes in the wider world. These are the companies that will fail. The world is changing faster than it ever, ever has, and the business world is becoming so fluid that statistics and analysis are at some stage going to be obsolete. The problems are not insurmountable, but they mean that if a person is running a business it is their responsibility to recognise and react in good time to external threats. It is not up to the government to bail out the whole of industry. The buck stops with the head of a company.

Like the wider economy, every business has a natural cycle, and there will be boom times and tough times. An entrepreneur should have some influence on this cycle by constantly finding ways to make their business go forward. It might be by searching for a different product or a new potential market, but the key is that they should always be looking to get better and better – or stop.

Taking the initiative

Statistics show that before the current recession more than half of small business start-ups failed within their first five years. Since the credit crunch took hold that figure has been steadily rising. In the first quarter of 2008 the number of companies going into administration was up 22.7 per cent on the same period the year before, and experts predict that the trend will continue at that rate through 2009 and 2010. With thousands of businesses just struggling to survive, entrepreneurs have had to face up to the idea of banks pulling the rug out from under them at any moment.

Indeed, since the credit crunch, stories abound of overdrafts being slashed and loans cancelled at a moment's notice, and this type of thing is capable of sending even a well-run business to the wall.

Of course, some businesses are making too many mistakes, and the banks genuinely have every reason to be nervous about them. However, the tragedy is that too many other well-run concerns are being caught up in these blanket decisions.

The key is to start talking to your bank early, even if there is absolutely no indication whatsoever that there might be a problem. Ask them, 'I am not defaulting, my business is cash positive, so am I at any risk of you withdrawing my loan in the future?' An entrepreneur should find out the bank's current criteria for lending money and if there is any danger that their business would breach those criteria. Be assertive and take control because it is much better to move your money when you don't have to than to do it when you have no choice.

Many business people are nervous about even raising the subject of lending criteria during tough economic times, believing that if they put their head above the parapet they will be vulnerable. Although I wouldn't recommend going in all guns blazing and demanding to know what is happening, it would be a crazy bank that penalised somebody with a sound business and a good track record who is being proactive and looking to the future.

You are the bank's customer, after all, and the least they can do is explain their situation. Banks can't fail to be impressed by someone who goes to them and says: 'I have not got a problem. I just need to know if you are going to cause me a problem.' That business will inevitably move to the top of their good investment list. Businesses that are keeping quiet are the ones they will be concerned about.

If, for some reason, the business suddenly moved out of the bank's lending criteria, I would urge entrepreneurs to do some research and find out what the criteria are at other banks. Find out who is lending money, because someone may be, and try to switch your loans to them. Ask the existing bank for a reference to give to the other bank – if a business has never defaulted and has a good cash flow it is perfectly reasonable to ask for references.

None of this is easy, but people often misunderstand what banks are. They are a business too, and their business is lending money. Banks have to keep doing it or they fail, so they will continue to be on the lookout for good lending propositions.

Even before the current economic turmoil the biggest single reason for business failure was an underestimation of the funding requirements and cash flow. Even the best-organised start-up, which has done everything by the book, with a well-researched market, an in-depth business plan and a fabulous product, will fail to judge how much money it will need. Many of my *Dragons' Den* investments have had to come back for more money, albeit on a short-term basis. Nobody gets it absolutely right.

Communicate with your bank *before* trouble begins

At the core of this underestimation of funding is a naive misunderstanding of cash flow. Business founders tend to believe that they will begin trading on day one, take X amount in the first month and Y amount in the second month. It never works like that. Whatever their trading terms are and no matter how forcefully they emphasise that fact, customers are going to push them back. Then, with money being paid in later, there is the double whammy of suppliers asking for payment up front because they are dealing with a new trader with no track record.

To compound the cash-flow horrors, the discrepancies often come as a complete shock to entrepreneurs, because, as we have already seen, bookkeeping has more than likely been put on the back burner while the entrepreneur gets on with the 'more important' stuff. With no one tracking the income, start-ups fall back on the comforting, yet totally misguided thought that they have loads of orders so they are bound to have loads of money.

I never accept a business plan at face value. If I am interested in investing in a company the first thing I do is something I call a 'sensitivity test', which basically says, 'What if?' This often involves knocking back the business-plan timing by at least two years. Entrepreneurs are often too optimistic. Their enthusiasm is fine and will stand them in good stead in the tough months ahead, but when it comes to cash flow and a fallback position they need to temper their optimism with some realism.

Overtrading – putting the focus too heavily on turnover rather than profit – is another common cause of failure. Too many entrepreneurs confuse the idea of success with how quickly they can grow their business. I am the last person to repress the potential success of a business by urging caution, but I would want a company to be absolutely certain that it was making profits before it made a move for significant growth.

Broaching the subject

No one really likes talking about business failure, even though it is precisely the time when it is trying to avert failure that a fledgling business needs more advice than ever before. Indeed, a quick Google-led search among the myriad entrepreneurial websites for advice on 'small business failures' will yield barely an acknowledgement of such a possibility. In fact, they are far more likely to focus on success while briefly trotting out such gung-ho platitudes as 'failure is not an option'.

Yet it is nothing to be ashamed of. Some of Britain's best-known businessmen have had some sort of significant failures along the way. Sir Alan Sugar, who built Amstrad into a multimillion-pound business from lowly beginnings selling car aerials and cigarette lighters, had some spectacular flops along the way. His attempt to enter the video gaming market in 1990 with an 8-bit GX4000 machine was completely eclipsed by the 16-bit Sega Megadrive. His emailer and videophone, which combined phone, video calling and emailing, also failed to capture the public's imagination.

Another business giant and one of the UK's most famous entrepreneurs, Richard Branson, started off failing with two teenage ventures to grow Christmas trees and breed birds. Over the years of expanding his ubiquitous Virgin brand, not all his ventures have been a resounding success and many do not seem to have got much further than the trademark showy opening ceremony.

But the point is, in both these examples and in countless others from established and well-known business executives, these successful and charismatic men got far more right than they did wrong. They were not afraid of jumping right in and trying something. They did, however, have an alternative plan if things did not work out as expected and moved straight on to make it happen.

It is this alternative plan which, I think, is key, and the onus is on the business to think ahead to when times might get tough. While it doesn't make sense to start a new venture by preparing for catastrophic failure, you should have a space in your plan for how the business will react if things do go wrong. The problem is that most entrepreneurs are eternal optimists, who keep thinking they can make it work. Even while all the signals show that there is a real problem, they live in a constant state of denial and are extremely unlikely to dig out the plan of what to do in the event of difficulties, let alone ask for advice.

One of the biggest problems is that by the time most businesses begin looking for people to talk to, they are not really seeking advice but are actually looking for help and comfort. They may even realise that it is, by now, too late and that only a magic spell can turn their business around. They are looking for someone they trust and respect to do the equivalent of an adult putting their arms around a child when they scrape their knee and telling them it will be all right.

Sometimes when someone begins to wake up to the fact that they are going to have to do something quite unpleasant, such as fire people or reduce spending dramatically or even take the

Get advice fast

decision to close the business down, pride can get in the way. It is much easier to talk to someone who says it will be fine and that it is the market's fault, not theirs. If and when people come to me for advice at this stage, I always ask them to explain to me, in detail, the intricacies of the business and how they got to where they are today. Until they do this, any platitudes from an adviser are just meaningless.

Although it can be difficult to do, setting it all down on paper and analysing where it went wrong is quite revelatory. Often, if they go through this exercise the person seeking advice will not actually need any help at all because, by listing it all, point by point, it becomes glaringly obvious what needs to be done. Of course, the answer may not leap out, but the process of saying 'This is what has happened to my business, and these are the factors that have had an effect' means that any advice the company does get will be far better targeted and advisers will know considerably more about what sort of advice is required.

Occasionally, instead of asking directly for advice, entre- preneurs might say to people they respect and trust, 'I am thinking of doing this to get the business back on track. What do you think?' That would be a much more proactive thing to do, and successful businesses always know how to be proactive. Too many people look for somebody else to do it for them. Now more than ever, when a business is in serious difficulties the entrepreneur should be in control and taking responsibility for their actions.

If there are investors on board, a failing business has to give them some consideration too, because it will quickly reach a stage where they are likely to start spending investors' cash to keep the business afloat as well as burn through their own capital. People are often not honest enough with their investors, and they find it difficult to tell them when things are tough. They think it will send an investor into a panic. Well, nothing will send an investor into a panic more than someone saying for months that everything is fine and there are no problems at all, and then suddenly popping up with the news that the company is down £100,000. That will send any investor into a tailspin.

Often it is the moment that the cash finally runs out that drives entrepreneurs to confess the true situation to their investors. If the investors are friends and family it can be a salutary moment, but unfortunately, loved ones will often opt to pump in another £10,000 or so to keep the company afloat. This is another reason for cautioning against such a relationship. An investor is more likely to ask searching questions about the real state of the business, such as why it has run out of cash and why it has taken so long for the entrepreneur to reveal the seriousness of the situation.

This does not mean entrepreneurs need to be on the phone to an investor every day, revealing that they have just lost an order for, say, £1,000. No. But they should be calling with the big news, the headline figures. An investor is comforted when they are working with a company that understands its market well enough to know when to say that the next year is going to be difficult. If the company says that it may well have zero profits this year and could even be down as much as 5 per cent on the previous year but is doing X, Y and Z to get things back on track, an investor will be forgiving. If I were in the entrepreneur's position I would be absolutely honest about what might or might not happen with the business and give an investor a realistic range of what the business is expected to do.

A company should, however, always be realistic in its expectations of an investor. People get confused about the differences between investors and directors. Investors put their money into a business and expect the person behind that business to run it efficiently and deliver a return on the investment. There should be no assumption that, when times are tough, experienced investors are going to wade in, roll up their sleeves and solve all the problems at a stroke. Look at it from the other viewpoint. How frustrating would it be for you if, once you had secured money from investors, they were there fiddling around with the idea at every opportunity? It is an investor's job to find a good idea and invest in it – that is all. However, if a business has chosen an investor carefully and that investor has a good track record and a background in the relevant market, it would be right and proper to ask for advice at a time like this. I would far prefer that my investments used my knowledge in this way, rather than languishing in silence until it is too late. But no matter how much help and advice they seek from their investors, entrepreneurs should remember that it is the directors who run the business and who are ultimately responsible for the decisions made within it. Seeking advice is good, but the real trick is knowing what is good advice and acting on it.

Taking the decision to quit

With bills piling up and banks and creditors knocking at the door, some business owners will spend their last penny pursuing a dream that has clearly turned into a nightmare. Some people do not spot the signs, and others just refuse to quit.

I once read a helpful article by a business commentator that likened the experience to a smoke detector going off in a house. The normal reaction, when the klaxon is blaring and the house is filling with smoke, is to run away as fast as you can. Sadly, though, all too often businesses ignore the shrill screech of the alarm and put off their escape until it is far too late and it is inevitable that they will get burned.

The only reason to attempt to hang on to a business that is obviously failing is if it is possible to identify what has been done in that business to make it fail – to find, if you like, the source of the fire that is making the alarms ring. If entrepreneurs are still clinging on to 'outside circumstances', imagining that the market will pick up at any moment and it is all going to be all right, they are dreaming. They are simply not close to accepting that there is something rotten in the business itself.

If it has been a good business and it has failed even though there is a market for the product, it can only be down to one reason: the person at the head of that business. They have not changed or seen a change in the market, or they have failed to introduce enough new products. There is no point struggling on, believing that something from the outside will 'rescue' the venture.

It is not a sign of dedication, fortitude and loyalty to stick with a flawed and struggling business. Sometimes entrepreneurs just have to call it a day, just as I did with my ceramics and glass company. Remember, though, that if it's handled properly failure is not fatal, and a good entrepreneur will bounce back and even

Know when to quit

go on to far greater and more lucrative things. Even US invest-ment guru Warren Buffett walks away from unsuccessful stocks now and again. The notion that an entrepreneur should hang in there until the bitter end is insane.

What is perhaps the most difficult thing of all is calling the exact moment when it is time to walk away, and this is often hard to judge when so much hard work and emotion are tied up in the business. I would say that one of the keys to my success is the fact that I have always known when to quit. A lot of people in business do not, but a true entrepreneur will be able to see the bigger picture, be brutally honest and admit their own failures.

Obviously, the best course of action is to avoid trouble at all costs, and that means being constantly aware of the warning signs. If an entrepreneur is plugged in to the market or the accounts team is perceptive there should never really be any circumstances beyond a business's control that are powerful enough to send it to the wall. Take late payers, for example, who are often blamed for business failures. If a business is genuinely aware of its customers and the environment, there is no way that late payment could become a make-or-break issue. If a customer has always paid on the button of 28 days and then suddenly slips back two weeks and then to four, alarm bells should start screeching. Don't ignore them and certainly don't keep supplying the customer on the same terms, if at all. Business terms simply should not go from 28 to 60 days overnight.

A common mistake is to assume that even when a regular customer is clearly in trouble the previous good relationship will mean that there will be no adverse effect on the businesses connected with it. For some reason, firms will not countenance the fact that they may fall to the back of the queue. Actually, businesses go bust every day, harming people that they have worked with for a long, long time. Whatever the reasons and whatever the relationship, there is nothing they can do about it. If they have gone bust, they have gone bust and they don't have the money to pay people with whom they have always had good relationships. The key is to spot when the writing is on the wall and get out of the way before the dirt flies.

If people start behaving in abnormal ways, a company should ask itself why and draw its own conclusions, and it might then stop supplying them or change their terms or simply sell elsewhere. In addition, don't ever get to the stage where your business's success or failure relies entirely on the patronage of one main customer. If that customer is looking shaky or even decides to buy elsewhere, their supplier is doomed. Always spread your business.

As noted earlier, keeping accurate management accounts and reviewing them in detail on at least a monthly basis is incredibly important. For the day-to-day running of the business there should be a 'dashboard' or an 'at-a-glance' sheet of the most important figures in the business. I would set up the systems so they are available for a regular weekly review, possibly daily if needed, and make sure a cash forecast is included on this sheet, taking into account any possible non-payments from customers.

It is vital to know every aspect and angle of the cash-flow situation because another incentive to react quickly is the fact that, under UK law, if an insolvent company is trading a director may be liable for wrongful trading. If directors know, or should have known, that a company could not avoid becoming insolvent but still continues to trade, they must cease trading immediately and take steps to liquidate the company.

If, having reviewed the business, cash flow and the market and doing everything they possibly can, business founders still find the marketplace saying that things aren't going to work, they should pick up their marbles and go on to the next game.

Entrepreneurs should always be on top of things, even if it is the heart-breaking moment they decide to wind up their company. They need to know what is going to happen, put measures in place to make them happen as smoothly as possible and be utterly in charge of the process. When I discovered that everything had started to go wrong with my first business – when I noticed the orders drying up – I was completely honest with my two employees at the time. It was important to me that they understood the position, and the moment I realised that the writing was on the wall I advised them to find more secure jobs elsewhere. I made virtually no money from the venture, but I did not lose any, and I did not owe anyone a penny when I walked away. Most importantly, I have been able to use the valuable lessons I learned in that year in every other business I have ever been involved with since.

Winding up the business

What are the options for entrepreneurs once they have accepted that their company is in financial crisis? Step one should be to seek immediate professional advice, because there are a number of options and moving ahead can be quite complicated. It does not absolutely follow that a business will find itself the subject of insolvency proceedings, because some solutions are aimed at helping the company survive.

The two possible ways that a company may survive are administration and a company voluntary arrangement. Administration is a legal procedure that gives a company breathing space to take stock of the situation and restructure. The business founder has to apply for this procedure through the High Court and work with an administrator to deal with creditors. All the company assets will be protected to enable a plan of action to be put in place.

A company voluntary arrangement allows a company that is in serious financial trouble to try to work with suppliers to find an informal arrangement to make the company solvent once again. Creditors will be asked to accept a reduced amount, which will be paid back over a period of one to five years. Although this can be tricky to pull off, it can be in a supplier's long-term interests to make sure that the companies it works with continue to trade. It is also possible to take a more formal approach by applying to a court and appointing an authorised insolvency practitioner to get the process going.

Alternatively, there are two main ways to wind up a company. In the first, a charge holder, usually a bank, will appoint a receiver to assess the worth of the business and do a sum-of-the-parts type valuation of how much could be made by selling off all, or parts, of the company. A receiver's purpose is to recover the cash owed to the original charge holder, so often it will encourage the company to carry on trading to realise its assets.

Finally, if the business is insolvent – in other words, if it has completely run out of cash or assets to pay off any debts or money due to suppliers – liquidation is the most likely result. A liquidator will be brought in to wind up the affairs of the business and shut it down. It is the liquidator's job to make sure that contracts have been completed, any legal disputes are resolved, assets are sold and any outstanding money owed to the failed company is collected. The last part of this process is to dissolve the company and strike it from the Companies House register.

A company that is still solvent but that can see the writing on the wall can also elect to put itself into voluntary liquidation to shut the company down. These are not pleasant issues to talk about, and it is certainly the case that business people prefer to avoid the topic, but I believe it is important to know what the options are if you are going to make the right decision.

As well as facing the emotional wrench of shutting down a business, entrepreneurs will also be full of fear and trepidation about what the process will mean to them in personal financial terms. If they are a director of a limited company that goes into liquidation they will lose what they put in and if they have made any personal guarantees, such as their house, they will forfeit those assets too. Sole traders who become insolvent may face personal bankruptcy too, with any assets that they own being shared out among creditors.

In many ways, winding up a company can be more complex than starting it in the first place. Apart from the legalities of the various options, there are also employees to consider, relationships with family and friends who may have originally lent cash, and dealings with business partners. It is not a decision that can, or should, be taken lightly, and I would urge any one in this situation to seek expert counsel at the earliest moment.

Learning from your mistakes

True business leaders are responsible for everything in their business and will never apportion blame elsewhere. If something hasn't worked, they learn from it, move on and take full responsibility. And this brings me to assumptions about how entrepreneurs should behave after closing a company that they have sacrificed so much for in the past.

In the United States entrepreneurs lose nothing in terms of reputation if they fail several times before making a business work. The process of starting up, folding and starting up again is part of the learning process. In Britain, on the other hand, the culture has traditionally been far less forgiving of business failure, although things are improving.

Entrepreneurs should be given the leeway and support to bounce back. I would hate to see entrepreneurial minds crushed by petty rules that say they should hide away with their shameful failure. That said, I would take an equally dim view of any entrepreneur who behaved badly about paying off loyal creditors only to start up another business with full funds just days later.

To help the process, the first step they should take before dusting themselves down and considering what to do next, or whether to begin another enterprise, should be to take a long, hard look at what went wrong in their last venture. Closing one company down and then starting another in its place without properly realising the errors that were made will not resolve the fact that the entrepreneur was not monitoring the original business properly or make up for an earlier lack of judgement.

And, until those problems are recognised, any subsequent business start-ups may well be heading for a fall.

What people don't like to see is risk-taking entrepreneurs clearly too arrogant to learn from their mistakes. Really big personalities who try to bludgeon their way through repeated mistakes can be disastrous. If they don't have the humility to accept their mistakes and learn from them, it's hard not to imagine that history will simply repeat itself.

With the right idea, business plan and a fresh attitude, however, there is a reasonable chance that a good entrepreneur will find new sources of finance and support. Banks, although shy of repeated failures, recognise that people in this situation know their market. After all, people who have tried and failed should be the least likely to make the same mistakes twice. I have never had a problem backing someone who has previously failed in a business as long as there is no evidence of serial failures or financial misconduct. The only way to learn how to run a business is to go and do it, and, as I know myself, things do not always work out. There is no substitute for the steep learning curve of experience, which can involve tough financial decisions and even going through the trauma of having to sack people. If you are prepared to accept your mistakes and learn from the difficult times, you will be prepared for better times ahead.

Take full responsibility and then move on

'Anything that can go wrong will go wrong'

This a myth that is so against my philosophy of life that I find it hard to imagine why it ever came to be uttered. To say that things 'just go wrong', as if there is a victim who has played no part in the problem or who has no control over events whatsoever, is inexcusable. We all play a key role in our destiny by making sure that the job is done properly, the issues are anticipated correctly, and the necessary actions are taken to avoid or mitigate loss. Things going wrong should not become an everyday part of life; if they do the entrepreneur needs to do some serious work to find out why and institute a change. Indeed, even if something is not going the right way I would expect the company to be reactive and to get it sorted out, not to get into a downward spiral and blame everyone else for the position in which it now finds itself. After all, we know entrepreneurs like to be in control and to get things right, but this does not mean they have to get everything right. They just need to get more right than they get wrong. That is the way to succeed.

Chapter 11
When is it time to sell up?

When I first started to work at Weststar my philosophy was that it would be my business until the day I decided to stop working, which would probably be in around ten years' time. Yes, I planned to build it and sell it, but that was never my priority. It would be just too distracting. To sell a business, there has to be a healthy business to sell. Any entrepreneur's first concern should be to build a thriving business. Then, if the plan is to sell in five or ten years' time, they should do a sense-check every so often about the long-term strategic plans.

Every entrepreneur should have an exit strategy, however, something to work towards. It does not have to be the sale of the business. It might, for example, be to have the business for the rest of your life and then pass it on to your children. That is fine. There just needs to be something that says what you are doing all this for. You have to know the endgame to make sure that all the big decisions that are made along the way lead you closer to that point.

Since I have been an investor in other people's businesses I generally look for an exit from my investments after three to five years. Every investor is different, of course, and I do constantly adjust my timing along the way and will stay in for longer if necessary. I don't actually have to recoup my money in that time, but it is important to say to the companies I get involved with that I am planning to exit in three to five years so that everyone knows where they are going. The entrepreneurs have to get themselves prepared for that point, and it is no use their starting on a complex 20-year project if they have to pay back an investor in two years' time.

My exit from these businesses does not have to be the same as the entrepreneurs' exit because they could buy me out. There just has to be a clear understanding that at the end of the agreed period we sell, I sell or we float on the stock market in order for me to get my cash back. If investors and entrepreneurs are not clear about each other's expectations it is like getting married and then suddenly discovering that you and your partner have completely different goals in life.

First, get your house in order

The best thing you can do to prepare yourself for a sale is to make sure that all the paperwork is in order when it comes to issues like agreements with business partners. In the heady, early days when so much is happening it is all too easy to forget some absolutely fundamental things, and I am always amazed by how many people go into business with each other without getting the terms down in writing. I always draw up shareholders' agreements with my business partners, even when, as has been the case in the past, they are members of my own family. It is a sort of family charter, if you like, that addresses key issues such as leadership, management and board structure, succession planning and management, the appointment and involvement of non-executive directors, and procedures for resolving disputes.

The agreements are important for two reasons. First, they force people to go through things step by step at the outset and clearly define the roles. Second, it also means that, heaven forbid, if and when things do go wrong there is a very clear prescription for what happens next. Ideally, if these matters are documented they will never need to be looked at, and there are many times when I rely on asking the question, 'Is that what we have agreed to do?'

It is when difficult questions arise that a well-thought-out written agreement comes into its own. Take, for example, such an emotionally complex subject as what happens when one party wants to sell and another doesn't. I would want to reach an accord far in advance of such an event, which can spell real danger for a business, with partners following different priorities. This is the main reason I did the Weststar management buyout deal with my parents. We hadn't yet reached the stage where our agendas had completely diverged, but it was clear that they were looking towards reaping the cash rewards of their work, whereas I wanted to put the cash back into the business and build it even more. I wanted to secure my future in the business, the one I was going to put my life into, and therefore I wanted to reap the ultimate rewards.

A situation like this has to be resolved, and it may well mean that one partner has to find the means to buy another one out or find some other means of releasing cash, such as persuading their family to turn their share into a loan in return for interest payments.

It took two years of discussion before I began serious talks with my parents about buying them out. Succession can be a difficult topic, particularly in a family business, and I admit it did get heated at times, but once we reached agreement that it was going to happen, it took about six months to finalise the deal.

Of course, some entrepreneurs are more anxious to keep the business in the family than to sell it on to the highest bidder. In these circumstances, planning for an orderly succession is, of course, essential. Up to 80 per cent of all businesses in developed economies are family-run, and in the UK family firms account for around half of the country's economic activity. Family firms bring their own rewards and commercial advantages, but to keep a family company on track generation after generation can require a complex juggling act that balances business strategy with personal relationship skills. Yet, although the route to succession is obvious for many family firms, one of the main mistakes these companies make in their long-term planning is not to be clear in their agreements. The problems arise when both parties believe they are agreeing to something, but in fact one party is hearing something different. That is why getting the agreement in writing is a good backup, because it lays the terms out unambiguously.

My parents were fortunate that they had capable daughters with a lot of business sense, but that was a lot to do with our upbringing and that does not always happen. After all, in the gene lottery there is no guarantee that a family will produce good

Plan for the future

leaders in every generation. The primary responsibility of the head of a family firm is to look after the business, and in turn the business will look after the interests of the family, and that means getting the right person to run the business. At some stage that might mean that the person who takes up the reins might well be someone who is not a blood relative.

Sentiment should not come into it. It might be that the member of the family who is hankering after the position is not yet developed enough for the role. They might be brilliant one day, but if the time is not right they should not be allowed to assume control. The person at the head of the business has to take a dispassionate view and decide who is the best person to take the company to its next stage.

For the younger members of the family, who are waiting to step up to bigger things, I have some advice that is based on my own experiences. As I have said before, it was a huge mistake for me to begin working for my parents after I left business college, and it soon became obvious that they would not recognise my worth in the business. I quickly made the decision to explore my own opportunities, and it was not until many years later, with several business ventures under my belt, that my parents came to me and asked me to join the family business. This time things were completely different. I could ask them, 'Why do you want me?' I was in a position to demand flexibility in my decision-making and to be paid the going rate. In their minds – and, to be honest, in mine too – I was no longer a little girl. I was now a valuable member of the team with a CV stuffed full of business experiences. I would advise everyone who is considering stepping into a family business to go away and do their own thing for a while, otherwise they will not know their worth and their family will not recognise their worth.

Succession planning in a family business is always a sensitive subject, and most companies leave it too late. One unhappy consequence of the delay is that the person in the number two role, who reports directly to the managing director, often believes that they are in line for the top job whether or not they are part of the founding family. There may never have been a plan to promote this person, and often they are not necessarily the right person to take over the business. Some people are born to be second in command, and they are brilliant at it, but they are not necessarily suited to step into a leader's shoes.

What I would avoid at all costs is letting that second in command believe that one day they will take over if it is clear that that will never happen. If another member of the family is subsequently promoted over their head, the business is clearly heading for a fall. The original leader has just guaranteed that the second most important person in the venture will walk away, just when the family firm needs them most.

Running any firm has its challenges, but keeping a family firm on track often requires a careful balance of business strategy and personal relationship skills. Corporate issues, such as share ownership and board structure, become far more complex and potentially threatening to the business when family members disagree, which is why it is vital to keep an open dialogue and make sure everyone is fully involved in all decisions.

Issues need to be addressed, agreed and documented, so if a conflict arises there is a way of dealing with it. The secret to keeping it in the family is, as with any business, to protect its future and with that future its values, purposes and principles. Best of all is to set out the terms from the start.

Next, watch the market

When I was at Weststar I received many offers to buy the business from venture capital companies that were looking to get into the holiday-park market and from trade buyers who wanted to expand their own operations. Most of the early offers were easy enough to ignore. Having bought the business from my parents I had made plans to grow it into the largest premier holiday-park operator in the South, and at that stage I anticipated that I would be in the business for at least another eight years.

But at some point a number inevitably grabs your attention, and the figure that caught my eye came from a trade buyer who was backed by a private equity house. It arrived in 2002, a particularly heady time, when money was cheap and every financier worth his salt was on the lookout for the next best thing. It was a great time to sell, and I wonder if we will ever see such times again. In future it might not be so easy to judge a good time to sell. The best thing you can do is keep an eye on the market and try to be aware of all recent sales in your sector and of issues that might be appearing over the horizon.

If you are still unsure about when to consider selling, my advice would be to think about your reasons for selling. Ask yourself, 'If I got X amount of money for the business would it make me want to go? Or do I want to work until I retire?' It is also useful to take a good look at the environment you do business in.

Identify whatever it is that would precipitate a sale, then keep your eyes open so you know whether your moment for a sale comes up sooner than you expected.

Always keep your price in mind

Of course, selling a business is not as straightforward as selling a pair of shoes. At Weststar, after that initial figure had piqued my interest, we entered into the lengthy and drawn-out process of due diligence. Four months into this process my alarm bells started to ring. I was becoming deeply uneasy about the ever-shifting nature of the completion statement, the list of all the figures that accountants use to adjust the final price. For example, in the holiday business some people pay fully in advance when they book their break, whereas others pay a 25 per cent deposit. So, if I were to sell Weststar in December I might have a pile of cash in my bank account that actually applied to holidays that would be taken next year when I no longer owned the park. To mitigate against this effect, the accountants drew up a completion statement that said I was going to be paid £xx, but because I had kept the forward-booking cash of £100,000, that sum would be deducted from the final price.

People always fall out over completion statements. They start with a headline price, and then the vendor or the person who is buying will say that they want it adjusted for A, B, C and D, and suddenly there are an enormous number of things to disagree on.

There are many legitimate adjustments, of course, but too often it can become a tool to reduce or barter over the price. I'd lost count of the number of times I had asked earnest-looking accountants and financiers to give me a straight answer to my question, 'What is the number on the cheque?' That was the only number I was really interested in, and they were welcome to use all the smoke and mirrors they liked and do what they liked above the final line of that completion statement, but I was not selling the business unless the terms and number on the bottom line were what we had first agreed.

Time after time my question was batted off, as if it was of no importance. So, there I was, sitting in my office in Exeter. It was late on a rather cold Friday night of February 2003, and deep in the pit of my stomach I had an uncomfortable feeling that would not go away. This whole process had gone on too long, and it was time to put a stop to it. I was not as experienced in negotiations as I am now, but I was beginning to suspect that this was about more than just the figures. After months of rigorous due diligence, experienced acquirers sometimes rely on the fact that company owners reach a point in the sales process where they are so committed to the sale that they have already mentally retired and spent their windfall. They are probably already even picturing themselves lazing on a sun-drenched beach somewhere in an exotic millionaires' paradise.

What my potential buyers had perhaps not bargained for was that I was never really one for lounging around – and I am no pushover. I was selling because the price was good, not because I wanted to stop working. On the contrary, Weststar was unfinished business for me, so the deal had to be really good to make me walk away from it.

I decided to trust my instincts, which were telling me that the time for negotiation had long since passed. I was even slightly annoyed at myself for having let it go on so long. I picked up the phone and told the head of the private equity team that we had talked enough. I reminded them that they had approached me and offered me the deal, not the other way round. My tone was matter of fact. I had not changed my position on the price one iota, whereas they had. The deal was either to be done at the original price, by midnight, or it would fall for good. If they came back with an offer that was just £1 less than what both parties had originally agreed, I would walk away. I concluded the conversation by adding that if they wanted to persist in chipping away at the price, they would do better to quit now and not waste any more time or money.

I received no response whatsoever, the deadline ticked over, and so I thought, 'Right, that's that,' and went into work the next day ready to get back to business as usual.

At 10.01 the following Monday morning, however, my phone gave a shrill ring. 'Hello,' said the overfriendly voice at the other end. Then, without waiting for a reply, my caller, the now erstwhile buyer, followed up with a business-like, 'So, what's happening?'

'Nothing,' I replied. 'Nothing at all. In fact, it is business as usual here, and there is not a single thing you could do or say that would change that.'

It does not sound much like a defining moment in my career, but it was. I was walking away from a deal worth many millions, and I still think of it as one of the best days of my life. It wasn't

Work out your cut-off point and stick to it

just that I felt I had 'won'. It was because I had regained the control that I had felt slipping out of my hands every time the process was drawn out a little longer. Before I allowed myself to become emotionally involved in the sale, I had privately decided my minimum price. I ignored the maximum, because in any deal there is no maximum. I didn't tell a soul what that minimum was, but I just decided what the figure was and knew I was not prepared to budge an inch.

If you ask most entrepreneurs what they would sell their business for they will always quote a top-end price – say £40 million – and it's usually clear that they have never even considered that it will end up below that sum. Pretty soon they are sucked into the process and realise that they are not going to get anywhere near £40 million, and they find it really hard to stop the selling juggernaut. That is how people end up getting far less money for their business than they wanted and find themselves feeling unhappy and frustrated. The further anyone gets down the process, the more difficult it is to walk away.

I decided to walk away when the price dropped by 2 per cent. Most people will think that that is not much in the overall scheme of things, considering that the deal was worth many millions, but I had made myself a promise about my bottom line. The potential buyer had reckoned that a drop of just 2 per cent would not be enough to make me walk away from the deal, but it was south of the line that I had drawn. What is the point of drawing a line if you are going to let yourself step over it?

I have to say that I have never regretted making that decision. Another extraordinary effect of killing the deal was that my actions buzzed through the leisure industry like wildfire. Neither party in the negotiation had spoken to anyone else about the deal, in keeping with our strict confidentiality agreements, but, as often happens, immediately afterwards the whole sector was alive with the news. It is perhaps hardly surprising that when I did my next two deals everything went a lot more smoothly. I was not messed around, and nobody attempted to change the price for one moment.

Finally, move on

Moving on from an entrepreneurial venture that has taken so much time and emotion can and does leave people with a serious sense of loss. Here is something that has defined them for many years and occupied their thoughts for their every waking moment, and suddenly there is just a hole. That feeling can be even deeper if the entrepreneur is retiring and has nothing to go on to.

In my own case at Weststar, when I did eventually sell the business two years after the deal described above failed, my exit was made easier on many levels. I was ready to leave. Although I loved every second of my time at Weststar, I felt that I had done my job at the holiday-park business and was ready for new challenges. I like change, I like things moving and evolving, and I instinctively knew that it was time for me to leave the company.

The transition itself was made easier because I actually stayed on at the business for some months after I sold it to Phoenix in 2005. The venture capital group did not have a chief executive in place to replace me immediately and asked me to continue doing the job until they recruited the right person. This is quite unusual, because normally a venture capitalist will have found a

management team to parachute straight in the moment the ink
is dry on the sale contract.

After agreeing to cover the post for up to six months I found
myself in the strange situation of getting up and going back into
my office as normal the day after I had sold the business. I didn't
feel any different, the staff didn't feel any different, and Weststar
didn't feel as if it was anybody else's business but mine. I was still
in control of the day-to-day running, and all that had changed was
that Phoenix had taken over the board.

I was in the middle of a major capital expansion at the
Sandford holiday park and simply reported back to Phoenix, just
as I had previously reported to my Weststar board. They were a
pleasure to deal with, asking sensible questions and coming to
quick decisions. I could not have asked for a better scenario.

After three months we found a replacement, and I moved to a
two-day week, a part-time role doing what I have always loved
doing, acquisitions. I visited 330 holiday parks across Britain in
the space of four months, meeting industry contacts and making
sure I knew what was going on. The other part of my new role was
business development, which meant seeing through the building
projects that I had previously started.

All in all, it was a nice, gentle exit and one that I thoroughly
enjoyed. I was proactive working at the business, and Phoenix
were very pleased with my continued commitment to the role.
I ended up staying on a part-time basis until I sold my remaining

23 per cent stake two years later. By that time I was doing very little at the parks and had become a Dragon, a welcome new challenge to stimulate my brain.

Eventually, it became obvious that it was time to walk away from Weststar, but I do think I would have found an instant exit quite difficult.

My advice to anyone considering a full exit is not to make too many plans. It is good to have something to fill that big hole in your life, but it is a fine balance too. If you want the deal to happen so badly because you have planned X, Y and Z, you will agree to almost anything to see it go through. In these circumstances you might suddenly find that you have given away £500,000 without thinking about it. But, at the same time, think about what you will be doing immediately after the sale because you will need to be doing something. Although there will be a feeling of triumph that your dream has finally been realised, it can be a massive anticlimax. Find a way to walk away from it and celebrate that you did it. You will deserve it.

'Look after number one'

Looking after number one is selfish and short-sighted. A company founder should look after everyone who is involved in their business and on the outside. Then the business will look after them. If an entrepreneur puts their own needs and wants ahead of the business and its requirements, particularly in the early days, they run a real risk of allowing the business to fail. It is a symbiotic relationship. A person who makes sure that a business gets what it needs will more than likely end up getting what they need out of it.

Afterword

Having invested in many businesses and rejected hundreds more, I like to think that I have quite a good insight into why some entrepreneurs succeed and others don't. Of course, the odd one gets away. There are a few entrepreneurs who have appeared on the *Den* I kick myself for not investing in. I am thinking particularly of Imran Hakin and his iTeddy, the interactive teddy bear with a computer in its tummy, which is designed to help preschool children learn while they play. The idea has gone on to be fabulously successful, and Imran has proved adept at finding other eye-catching ideas too. Overall, though, I like to think I have a pretty good batting average and that I have developed an eye for spotting talent.

In the Den, I am on the lookout for entrepreneurs who are prepared to think creatively and solve any problem that comes their way. I'm looking for people who have a thirst to make things just that little bit better. I am always questioning my motives for doing things; I am always thinking, 'What if we did it this way?' or 'What if we looked at it from the other angle?', and I like to throw questions at the pitchers in the Den to see if they have that same habit. If the would-be entrepreneurs can deal with these questions, then I know we're starting off on the right foot. If you want your business proposal to succeed then I would absolutely suggest that you consider these fundamental questions before you go any further.

1. Do I have the right personality?

No one has the perfect entrepreneurial profile, but there are some characteristics that show up again and again, including passion, confidence, intelligence and quick-wittedness.

2. Will I be able to deal with knock-backs?

You should not even consider starting a company unless you are physically and mentally resilient and in good general health. As well as having to roll with the punches of the inevitable setbacks of the early days, you will probably have to work for long hours, and you're bound to find it stressful.

3. Can I be honest at all times?

No one wants to work with people who are not upfront, honest and straight-talking. Whether it is a bank, a business angel, customers or suppliers, they need to know that the company they are dealing with is knowledgeable and truthful.

4. Am I prepared to take risks?

Entrepreneurs aren't afraid of taking a calculated risk and failing. They positively welcome it as part of the learning process. After all, if they don't push the boundaries, how will they ever find out what they are capable of achieving?

5. Is my vision strong enough that I will be able to see it through even when the going gets tough?

Having a good idea is great, but turning it into a business is not so easy. Entrepreneurs must have the vision not only to recognise the importance of the idea, but also to see a way of getting it to market. They need to be persistent and to stick to their guns if they are going to meet their objectives.

6. Have I done enough research and do I know my market?

Just because well-meaning friends say something is a good idea, it does not mean that it is. One of the biggest causes of business failure is neglecting to spend enough time researching the idea to see if it is viable or miscalculating the market size and potential market share. To do this, entrepreneurs must be constantly plugged into the market; they need to understand the zeitgeist and predict the flow. Something that bombed a few years ago might be all the rage today.

7. Am I prepared to plan carefully?

In the heady days of converting an idea into a business it is easy to underestimate financial requirements and timing and to overestimate sales projections. Getting every aspect of the business down on paper and objectively analysing all of the permutations in a structured plan is essential.

8. Can I adapt to changing circumstances?

To be successful you will need to recognise, and then leap on, new opportunities – even in the midst of misfortunes. Change is inevitable, and you will need to adapt fast enough to survive in a highly competitive business environment.

9. Am I self-reliant?

Business decisions, such as taking on new partners or extra staff, must be made on the basis of what the company requires. Your friends and family are there to support you, but when it comes to the business you need to recognise if they are becoming a distraction. If you hire for convenience, rather than skills, your business risks becoming overpopulated by people who cannot do their job well and are hard to get rid of.

10. Do I know when to delegate?

Entrepreneurs, by nature, like to be in control. This is a good trait, but it must be moderated when you are setting up a team. You must learn to control your desire to meddle in everything and, instead, get on with what you are good at.

11. Am I able to communicate my ideas and my message?

No product or service, however good, will sell itself. You have to find an effective way to tell potential customers about your product and give them a good reason to buy it. Now is the time to be short, sharp and punchy – people need to know exactly what you mean. There are a lot of voices out there, and you have to make sure people want to listen to yours.

12. Am I prepared to sell, sell, sell?

When you're starting your own business it is not the time to be shy. Even if you find selling difficult in the early days it should occupy about 80 per cent of your time. Any time left can be used for engine-room activities.

13. Am I focusing on the right things?

Focus is essential, but it must be channelled in the right way. Entrepreneurs should never lose sight of the fact that profit is their main reason for running a business and the means by which they can make further good decisions. Sales volume and company size are simply a means to an end.

14. Do I know where I'm going?

You must have long-term aims built into your plan, with targets for one, five and ten years ahead. Clarity of purpose is vital. It is fine to say a company is to remain a one-man band for good, but if the intention is to grow it into a multimillion-pound corporation you will need to put structures in place from the outset so that you can achieve that end.

Once you've thought through these questions, you should have a good idea of whether running a business is for you. Then it is simply a question of getting on and doing it – even in a recession. Since the onset of the credit crunch, countless would-be entrepreneurs have asked me if they should still start their business. The questions I fire right back at them are, 'How strong is your business? How strong is your idea?' If the business proposition is strong and the entrepreneur is prepared to adapt to current circumstances, it will survive. As I have said before, the rule book has been torn up, but those entrepreneurs who are prepared to take a new approach and think creatively can – and will – make their fortunes.

Setting up and running a company is not complicated, as I hope I have shown. All you need do is use your head, be focused and keep things simple. But you have to be prepared to work hard. Start-ups can be physically challenging and emotionally draining. As a company grows there will inevitably be periods when it is frantically busy and the adrenalin will flow. It's certainly not the easy option, but if you get it right, or even just mostly right, the rewards are far greater than the downsides. Apart from being fun, it is utterly thrilling to develop an idea into a serious proposition and watch it fly.

Appendix 1

Writing business and marketing plans

Throughout this book I have tried to emphasise how important it is for every entrepreneur to make a plan. Some people tend to think that plans are just a tool to get funding, but I believe they are an incredibly useful way for entrepreneurs to make sure they are always on track.

In order to get the most out of your business and marketing plans, it's important to write them properly, and here's a guide to getting them right.

Business plans

Executive summary

The executive summary is like the front page of a brochure, reflecting the key elements of why someone might like to invest in the business. It should be simple and no longer than a single A4 sheet. Although it appears at the front of the business plan, it is accepted practice to write it last, after the rest of the plan has been finalised.

If the purpose of the plan is to raise funds, the summary should say just that and lay out the terms clearly – for example, 'We are seeking to raise £1 million, we are prepared to give up xx per cent of the equity, and your return on the investment will be £xx.'

Do not get bogged down in the history of the business. The key is to grab the reader's attention, and the summary tells them why they should bother spending time reading through the rest of the plan. If it doesn't immediately get their attention, or they don't like what they read, they will read no further.

If I were writing an executive summary to raise funds for expansion at Weststar Holidays it would include something like:

> **Weststar Holidays operates five-star holiday parks throughout the South-West. The purpose of this plan is raise funds to accommodate a further three parks at the total cost of £xx million.**
>
> **The domestic holiday-park market is forecast to expand at a rate of 10 per cent per annum over the next five years, and we want to be best placed to take full advantage of this growth.**
>
> **Weststar Holidays is renowned for its marketing and has an exceptionally high response to its promotions, with an enviable conversion rate of 2 per cent.**

Summary

While many of the headlines contained in the summary will be the same as those in the executive summary, this is a much more detailed section, with a full description of the product or service. It will also add some indication of who the key competitors are and what differentiates this business from all the rest. This is the moment to showcase that the business really knows its market, its key competitors and avenues for growth.

So, to carry on with the previous example, an excerpt of this section would expand on the above information by saying something like:

> Figures from Recognised Industry Body Ltd show the holiday-park market is expanding at a rate of 10 per cent per annum over the next five years. At present the market is worth £xx billion per annum and divided among the following regions . . .
>
> Rising air fares, concerns over international terrorism and dwindling domestic budgets are encouraging record numbers of holidaymakers to stay in the UK. The South-West, where Weststar operates its five premium parks, is the single biggest destination for domestic tourism in the UK with xx million visitors annually, and Weststar has a xx per cent share of that market.
>
> The key areas of growth are seen to be in live entertainment and high-quality catering, which are two areas that are recognised as particular strengths in the Weststar group, which last year won awards for . . .

Product (or service) and operations

This section is where you detail how the product or service will be priced and what the margins are. You will need to address how the product or service will be delivered, who will be the key players and how much is being set aside to pay for key personnel.

You can afford to be very detailed here, and it's important that you format your document in a way that makes the key figures easy to find.

Sales and marketing plan

This is where you outline the desired market, including estimates of its size and details of any market research. First-time entrepreneurs, as I've mentioned before, have a tendency to overestimate the size of markets wildly, so it's worth getting some advice on this aspect from someone with experience of the industry. You'll also need to explain the sales and marketing strategies you intend to employ to reach the target market, and don't forget to include the size of the overall budget as well as details of the major expenses.

Technology

It is likely that some or all of your new business will be highly reliant on technology, which you will need to explain. It's important here to cover how the company has protected itself against down time or loss of data. It's also worth including any future developments or improvements that could be made through technology. Your potential investors will want to know how the company will keep its current systems relevant.

Financial plan

You will need to include a full cash-flow forecast together with what is needed for stock, payment terms against that stock, when the income is going to start coming in and when VAT and other tax commitments go out. Investors will also want to see profit-and-loss forecasts and relevant performance indicators, such as gross and net margins and wages as a percentage of sales. Those key performance indicators are personal to the business and should be made up of the figures that really show the health of the company.

Business funding

Here is where you show what assets the business plans to buy, where funding has come from to date, how much future funding is needed and where future money will be spent. Few people get this section right. There is a tendency to think of it as a load of words with no financial data, or financial data with no words. It should be a completely integrated section that gives a clear idea of the funding that is required.

Growth strategy

This is the section where you get to outline your plans for growth and development of the business in subsequent years, including a sales forecast, a cash-flow forecast and a projected profit for at least five years.

Exit options

It's worth taking the time to outline carefully the various routes to exit and to add realistic timescales. It can be helpful to draw up a list of the most likely acquirers, say why they would be interested and add a small amount of background information on each. You should also include any relevant market activity or interest where they may have invested in a competitor because this will strengthen your case.

Appendix

Finally, this is where you can include the CVs of the key management team, supporting research data and technical product information, financial sensitivity tests showing best-case and worst-case scenarios and any brochures or literature that will help demonstrate exactly what it is that the company is planning to do or is currently doing.

Marketing plans

Summary and introduction

This section is where you set out your stall and tackle what the plan is for, who it is trying to target and what it is trying to generate. The plan itself does not necessarily have to be concentrating on raising cash through marketing, but if it is, it should say how much and over what period. Alternatively, if you're going for brand awareness in order to make sure that, say, 5 per cent of the population get to know about the product, you should define that, too.

Although this marketing summary will appear at the beginning of the plan, it should be written last. Writing the summary is a good opportunity to check that the plan makes sense and that you haven't missed any important points.

External and internal analysis

This section gives you the opportunity to consider the environment in which your business operates. You should already have quite a good idea of this if you have done an analysis of your ideal customer. You should also consider, however, the external factors that might have an impact on the business, such as political or legal changes, economic factors, such as interest-rate changes, and technological factors, such as increased use of the Internet. Also, you should describe any weaknesses within the company, such as limited resources.

Objectives

This detailed breakdown of the marketing objectives should be specific and linked to business objectives. If, for example, the sector analysis shows the entire market is worth £500,000, you should consider how much income you can actually generate. There is clearly no point spending £1 million on a flash campaign if the potential market is half that size. That may sound obvious, but it is amazing how many people don't put a value on it. Most marketing plans that I see miss the outcome. They just say: 'We are going to advertise here, do some PR there, do this and do that and it is going to cost X amount.' Instead, what they should say is: 'This product is trying to generate £100,000 in sales, so the business is going to spend £2,000 to get there.' It might also say that it is setting aside £1,000 on brand awareness for the long term.

At Weststar, I might have included something like:

We want to generate £10 million in holiday sales income next year, an increase of 15 per cent on last year. We're going to spend £1 million on marketing to achieve this. This represents an increase of 20 per cent on last year's marketing budget but will achieve a return on investment (ROI) of 1:10.

Then – and this is absolutely vital – you need to include a scheme showing how the company is going to track whether the plan is a success. This will enable you to assess whether the strategy works or, if it doesn't, why it failed. Was it the wrong format? Did the advertisement appear on the wrong day? Without this feedback the exercise is virtually worthless, and the company might accidentally forget to repeat something that generated 30 per cent of its revenue. One strategy for tracking the effectiveness of marketing activity is to use a source-code system. At Weststar, when we placed an advert in a paper or sent out a mail shot, we would give that activity a code which we would incorporate into it. The bookings team were then trained to ask the customer for this code when they took a booking, and we were able to run reports to see how many bookings each piece of marketing activity generated.

Strategy

Now that you know the customer and understand the market, what can you offer to attract these people? How can you secure a competitive advantage? This is the part of your marketing plan where you set out your programme for getting people to sit up and take notice.

One idea it to partner up with like-minded businesses and offer discounts. A children's entertainer, for example, might team up with a party-bag supplier, and together they could offer a 10 per cent discount on all bookings.

Marketing tactics

In this section you should set out how you plan to make the strategy a reality. Marketing people call this the four Ps: Product,

Pricing, Place and Promotion. In its simplest terms, it is the section that says how the product meets the customers' needs; the level at which the pricing will be set; how and where the product will be sold; and the way the company will promote itself to the final consumer, whether it is advertising, PR, direct mail or personal selling.

Timetable

Just as there is no point in spending lots of money on a campaign with little potential for return, so it is important not to waste time on overelaborate marketing schemes. You will need a timetable that will clearly set out each step that will be taken to make sure that the marketing plan is fulfilled, with timelines and key tasks. It is really important to consider carefully how long it will take to produce a brochure or design a website and build this into the plan.

Appendix 2

At-a-glance common sense rules

The aspiring entrepreneur

Seek out opportunity and seize it

Entrepreneurs need to be plugged into their sector so that they can spot gaps and step in at the right time with the right product.

Spend your time wisely

Rather than spending hours comparing experiences and swapping tales of doom, I would much prefer to see people just getting on with it.

Nothing is impossible

There is always a way, and everything can be done. Unless it is actually against the laws of physics, it should be possible to find a route.

Take calculated risks – don't gamble

If you have done your calculations in a cool-headed and realistic way and still believe the risk is worth it, it probably is.

Enjoy yourself

Nobody can force that feeling of enjoying every challenge – and if you don't, why should you keep on doing it day after day?

Turning great ideas into great businesses

Brilliant ideas are good, but brilliant business propositions are what count

Sadly, millions of great ideas fall by the wayside every year because they don't get taken any further. Entrepreneurs need a business proposition that says: 'I have had this idea, this is why I am the person to exploit it, and this is the way I will go about it.'

Give your product an edge and then tell everyone about it

What makes this idea different? Is it offering anything unique? Does the person behind the idea have any special skills or expertise? Is the business focused on a niche segment or on the mass market? Is there anything special about the way you are planning to do business? Answer these questions with complete honesty, and I guarantee a clear picture will emerge.

Don't get too hung up on confidentiality and patents

If people get tied in knots being protective about their business concepts there is a danger that these ideas will never actually get off the ground. Simply discussing the nature of the business with someone or showing rough plans is unlikely to be commercially sensitive.

Tracking down the investment you need

Business plans should be simple and concise

A business plan should be a step-by-step document that outlines timescales and milestones, what has to be done in the run-up to the launch and what it is going to cost. It should tell the investor in a punchy way what the business is all about, where it is going and what it needs to get there.

Consider the *business* reasons for going in with friends and family

Financial ties with relatives or friends may seem uncomplicated at first, but they can easily get extremely thorny. It is not always the case that knowing someone well or being related to them is a good basis for running a business.

Only pursue an investment that is right for you

Entrepreneurs should remember that they are choosing the investor in the same way that the investor is choosing them. They may well come out of their first meeting thinking, 'Hang on a minute, I have something here,' and that will give them much more ammunition when they go to other investors.

Pitches don't need to be perfect, just credible

I don't want to invest in somebody who is good at pitching; I want to invest in somebody who is good at business.

The all-important start-up phase

Business valuations should be realistic

Valuing a start-up with a catch-all formula is far too simplistic. The process is part science and part instinct, but to get a realistic view a significant amount of market and deal knowledge is essential.

Accept responsibility

The set-up phase of every venture is rather like having a baby because the business is completely dependent on the founder as its life source. If the entrepreneur does not stay ahead of what the business needs at all times, it will flounder.

Get the business covered

The one essential that is most often overlooked in setting up a business is insurance. It is horrifying just how unprepared most start-ups are for the unexpected.

Don't get hung up on names or status

Of course, entrepreneurs should be concerned about the impression their company will make, but spending hours agonising over what they should call it is a waste of time.

Always be honest with an investor

I make it clear with all my investments that I expect to be consulted directly if there is a problem. If something is not right, pick up the phone, set out what is wrong and let's find a way to fix it.

Alternative ways to start your own business – or turn someone else's around

Get the facts fast and keep the pace up

If your mind is made up, it is important to keep the negotiations moving on at a respectable pace. Time does kill deals.

Identify the strengths – and build on them

All businesses, no matter how badly they have been run in the past, will have some good qualities that customers liked. The trick is to find them – and fast.

Give the key people a reason to stay

If key people leave, the business will lose an important part of its fundamental character, making the task of successfully re-launching it even harder. There is a short window to get hold of the business and prevent this from happening.

Leading the way

Know what to spend your time on and when to spend it

Time management is a skill that few people get right and every-one can improve upon. I find it helps to set in my mind how long a task is going to take before I get started. It is surprising how many people don't do that.

Cash will not just flow – it needs to be managed

Managing cash flow is not something that will just happen in the day-to-day working of the business. It needs to be a business priority, particularly during the tough part of an economic cycle.

Set realistic goals

Realistic goals are one of the best ways to avoid feeling over-pressurised. When entrepreneurs get stressed out they find it hard to stay motivated, and this can be fatal to a fledgling business.

Resist greenwashing

I think it's great that the environment is now 'fashionable', because I do believe that it deserves more attention, but the downside is that some companies see it as an opportunity to jump on the bandwagon when they actually have little interest in or knowledge of the real issues.

Being ethical is not an indulgence

Some start-up companies have claimed that they can't afford to be ethical or environmentally friendly, but building these principles into the company from the outset can often save money.

Managing a talented team

Nobody works best alone

Finding the right people to work with can be difficult, particularly, it seems, for entrepreneurs, who tend to be rather keen on being in control and fearful of letting go of some of their precious venture. They will, of course, have to overcome this fear in order to take the business forward.

Remember to listen

The person at the top has to understand the ebb and flow of a business, and find a way to communicate and inspire the team at all levels. When you've put together a talented team it makes sense to listen to what they have to say.

Adopt a zero tolerance approach to bullying

Most people think bullying happens only within an organisation. It doesn't. It happens a lot everywhere in business, and it is up to a company manager to keep an eye out for it.

Tackle employment changes fast

If there is no option but to cut jobs, redundancies should be handled sensitively and carefully, and it's important that the company always operates within the legal framework.

Focusing on your brand

Marketing on its own means nothing

Marketing is all about getting the message about your great product out to the right people. When companies tell me 'We are a marketing driven business', I immediately become sceptical.

Build an *effective* online presence

Too many websites are badly designed. New businesses should put themselves in their potential customers' shoes. What would they expect to land on and see? What is it that they are looking for? And, above all, how are they going to buy?

All publicity is *not* good publicity
If any of the companies I invest in agree to interviews, I always ask them to write down three messages that they want to get out there and make sure that that's what they do.

Maximising sales

Nothing sells itself
Potential purchasers need a reason – and a good reason at that – to buy the product.

Value is the main consideration in pricing
Remember, value isn't necessarily financial. It is whatever importance the customer attaches to that product. To steal a march on its competitors a business has to understand the basis on which customers are valuing a product and aim to be the best in that area.

Sell them something they want and they will come back for more
People always say to me that it is difficult to speak to a buyer – and yes, it is difficult – but don't forget that a buyer's job is to buy products. If your product is right for them you should be able to strike a deal.

Customer complaints are an opportunity
If businesses can turn customers with complaints round and impress them in a personal way, those customers will be invaluable ambassadors for the company.

Keep existing customers happy

It costs much less to retain a customer than it does to acquire one, which is why it is a huge mistake to spend time and money acquiring customers only to upset them by virtually ignoring them thereafter.

Make sure your website delivers

When potential customers visit a company's website they should come away with the feeling that they have found exactly what, if not more than, they wanted.

When times are tough

Communicate with your bank *before* trouble begins

Many business people are nervous about even raising the subject of lending criteria during tough economic times, believing that if they put their head above the parapet they will be vulnerable. Although I wouldn't recommend going in all guns blazing and demanding to know what is happening, it would be a crazy bank that penalised somebody with a sound business and a good track record who is being proactive and looking to the future.

Get advice fast

No one really likes talking about business failure, but when a fledgling business is trying to avert failure, it needs more advice than at any other time.

Know when to quit

It is not a sign of dedication, fortitude and loyalty to stick with a flawed and struggling business. Sometimes entrepreneurs just have to call it a day.

Take full responsibility and then move on

If you are prepared to accept your mistakes and learn from the difficult times, you will be prepared for better times ahead.

Selling up and moving on

Plan for the future

Every entrepreneur should have an exit strategy, something to work towards. That way you can make sure that all the big decisions that are made along the way lead you closer to that point.

Work out your cut-off point and stick to it

Before allowing themselves to become emotionally involved in the sale of their business, entrepreneurs should privately decide their minimum price. They can ignore the maximum – in any deal there is no maximum – but they should decide what their bottom line is, and then stick to it.

Don't lose sight of why you started the business – and why you're selling it

Moving on from an entrepreneurial venture that has taken so much time and emotion can and does leave people with a serious sense of loss. But it is important to recognise when you have achieved what you set out to do and when it is time to move on.

Index

Deborah Meaden

Successful UK businesswoman and entrepreneur Deborah Meaden is best known as one of the dragons from BBC2's hit show *Dragons' Den*.

She's had an extremely successful career in business, starting out at the age of 19 with her own glass and ceramics import company, moving on to run one of the first UK franchises for Stefanel, an Italian footwear and clothing firm, and eventually joining the family company, Weststar Holidays. She staged a management buyout in 2000, and in 2007 sold the business in a deal worth £83 million, giving her the freedom and capital to invest in new opportunities.

Her *Dragons' Den* investments range from MixAlbum, an automated music mixing system, and Magic Whiteboard, a product that combines the best of a flipchart and a whiteboard, to yoodoodoll, a doll that you can make resemble anyone you like (or dislike).